*"Good morning! I'm not sure if I have the right person, but I'm looking for Jonny Burgess who wrote 'You Can Too'. You spoke at our Kick-off 3 years ago. I got your book, applied what you wrote, and saw fantastic results. If you are him, could you let me know?"*

**—DSC Stacy C. (Colorado)**

*"Thank you very much for the information. I believe out of all the speakers we have had, your talk made the most sense to me in terms of how to do this job and take control of your life…"*

**—Michelle M. (Connecticut)**

*"Just wanted to show you my results so far this year by using your methods. $105,062! Best year ever in my insurance career! Thanks again for your encouragement with your book."*

**—Mike T. (Georgia)**

*"I've read it too. It's a great read. A lot of good information. It's worth the $ to buy it as an iBook."*

**—John W. (DSC)**

*"It's an easy read, You can read it in a few hours. I think it's a must read for ANY Aflac agent…It's good to know what works for others and you may just find that one golden nugget of information that you can strike it rich with. I've read it a couple times, and it DOES work. And let me say this, if you're struggling then it's a must read."*

**—Dale T.**

*"Just hit Fast Start…thanks for the words to say!!! Your plan just flat works!!!!"*

**—Dave R. (North Carolina)**

*"Jonny, thank you for telling your story at the Syracuse Regional meeting for Joe Colarco in July. I have read your book twice and I am getting lots of appointments…I have been with Aflac for 9.5 years and it was getting to be not so fun, but this has made it fun again, so thank you,"*

**—Jim B. (New York)**

*"I've read it. It's a quick read with lots of great ideas. Just check out Burgess on RPM, his numbers prove that he knows what he's doing, he's a Rockstar! I read the book, applied it, and it made prospecting so much easier! You look at it differently. Easy way to help those little shops that need the accident plan, no brainer! Every new associate needs to read the book"*

**—Carrie C.**

*"I read the book and it has a lot of great tips and helpful information on how to get started. How to earn some money quicker, and how to PACE with a clear purpose."*

**—Dana B.**

*"Read it…Loved it. Quick read with great info."*

**—Yolanda**

*"I've read it, and found it to be practical and useful. Very quick read, and gives great ideas and a different perspective."*

**—Kathy B.**

"*I ran a test pilot with a couple agents using your system you wrote about. The results were fantastic, both in success and excitement! I am having a meeting with all of my new agents on Tuesday the 22nd and am going to roll out your book to them. Was wondering if you could send us any words of encouragement or advice. Also, would love to get our team copies of your book autographed at FOCUS if possible. Thanks again for sharing your stories and methods!*"

**—Steven H. DSC (Victoria, Texas)**

"*This has been the best year ever for me. I followed a lot of your advice in your book. I have $88,139AP YTD. I have qualified for VIP Bonus 3rd QTR and 4th QTR! I really didn't apply your concepts until mid-year. But it has worked, I've opened groups, and got my eye on about 12 others. Recruited some folks with the ABC program, and have a 300-man group to open in January. Thanks!*"

**—Mike T. (Franklin, Georgia)**

"*I actually gave the book to some of my agents-great information. Great 'How-To' book.*"

**—Larry H.**

"*Thank you so much for writing your book...Tuesday we wrote our first enrollment. I feel confident and competent that by the end of this week, I will be able to run the process and enrollment, all because of your blueprint. Once again...Thank you!*"

**—Jay J. (Toledo, Ohio)**

"Hi Jonny, just wanted to reach out and thank you so much for educating us at our regional meeting last Monday. You make it sound so simple, which I guess it really is. Most of us tend to overthink things and make them too complicated. James & I used your script today in PACE and got 5 appointments. Can't say why it's working, but we did the 'rewind/play' thing over and over, and were naïve enough to believe...thanks for taking the time out of your busy schedule to try and help us all. I hope we all appreciate it, I know I do." Warmest regards,

**—Dawn P. (Utica, New York)**

"Jonny, thank you for putting your book out there! Just to update you, I'm getting appointments pretty much every time I go prospecting. I did 3 groups just last month using your script. I have never had this much fun prospecting and am getting appointments like never before. They all don't pan out, but because there are so many appointments, it's a numbers game to turn over so many to become accounts. I realize now that I had been giving out too much info and complicating things... Thanks again and have a great day!"

**—Jim R. (Norwich, New York)**

# YOU *STILL* CAN TOO

Take Your Aflac Career to a
Whole New Level!

## JONNY BURGESS

BONUS: Building a Million Dollar District in a Year

STONEWALL PRESS

PAVING YOUR WAY TO SUCCESS

Published in the United States of America

ISBN: 978-1-64460-013-9 (*sc*)
      978-1-64460-012-2 (*e*)

Library of Congress Control Number: 2018959508

Published by Stonewall Press
4800 Hampden Lane, Suite 200, Bethesda, MD 20814 USA
1.888.334.0980 | www.stonewallpress.com
1. Business
2. Guide
18.10.24

*This book is dedicated to my beautiful wife, Michelle. You believed in me when I was a broke, single father of five children, starting all over again. You believed in me even before you had a reason to.*

*We blended our families, had all eight of our kids under our roof together, and lived our life "in-the-blender", but we made it work. We've had our ups and downs, emotional highs and lows... and we're still standing!*

*There's nobody I want by my side as I conquer "my 100" more than you, no-one I'd rather travel and explore the world with.*

*Thanks for your patience as I spend countless hours in the hot tub visualizing and planning our outrageous future together, and the countless hours in the field making it a reality.*

*Few find their "soul-mates" in this world. I'm grateful to God that I did!*

# Contents

# Introduction

*"Good morning Mr. Burgess, I am praying you are the author of the wonderful book on Amazon. (If not I am sure you get these notes frequently). If you are indeed Jonny B., my most sincere thanks for a wonderful book. It has influenced my new career with Aflac immeasurably. I am 63 and street legal now for 1 week. But my first week out I booked 12 appointments!"*

—David R. (North Carolina)

I HAVE TO START out by expressing my extreme gratitude to the overwhelming response to my first book, "You Can Too". To this day, I get countless e-mails saying, "Are you the guy who wrote the book?" And to this day I do my best to personally call back every one, and many times coach over the phone, agents from Alaska to Cape Cod Massachusetts. I've addressed countless Districts and Regions, via Skype or in person, and many Monday Morning Meetings. I believe I've actually spoken in 21 states at either a training, a kick-off or other event.

I am (humbly) proud to say that the #1 account openers in countless Markets and Regions are proponents of my

"You-Can-Too system". I get such a feeling of satisfaction seeing all the names on RPM…knowing that I personally helped propel individuals to success in this business.

The success I talked about in my first book has absolutely continued to increase, year after year, and I live in a state of gratefulness for the lifestyle I am able to enjoy. From flat broke 9 ½ years ago, to a million-dollar net worth in 8 years. We are leaving for our Territory Convention to Miami in about 7 weeks, and that will be my 114th vacation in less than a decade. Crazy right?! From Italy 3 times, to Cannes France, Barcelona Spain, a private Sheryl Crow concert in Hawaii, countless cruises (I bet at least 10), Disney World multiple times, the Dominican Republican twice, a Cowboy ranch trip in Arizona, dog sledding in Whistler Canada. From Vegas to riding a Mardi Gras float in New Orleans. Mexico multiple times, twice to Costa Rica, several ski resorts, a trip to Nashville, seeing the NCAA Final Four live in Houston. From Bar Harbor Maine to the Riverwalk in San Antonio. Then add in dozens of camping trips, and most recently 'glamping'.….camping at my favorite resorts…like Bayley's in Old Orchard Maine that has 6 hot tubs! (It's honestly a little ridiculous).

My administrator Allie bought me a plaque that states "Work Hard Play Hard" that now hangs in my office. I do both very well!

But remember, the entire theme of my first book is that "You Can Too!"

And here's the best part. My success is a direct result of helping countless other people. I've been able to bring countless other people along with me, and at the same time provide a bedrock of security to my clientele. My customers 'know' that Aflac will absolutely be there in their hour of need should an unexpected crisis hit their family.

I am so blessed to have discovered that commission sales is now by far the highest paid profession in this country… passing both doctors and lawyers years ago. It saddens me that so many people choose the 'security' of a $1000/week paycheck when they can make that (or much more) in a single day in this business. And (the coolest part), collect renewals for years and years to come for work they do today.

There are certainly many things you can sell…from copiers to food, to houses to Kirby vacuums. But then again, I don't feel like you are really impacting the customer's life a whole lot by selling them a $2000 vacuum (after cleaning 'part' of every room in the house). I bought one years ago partly to get rid of the guy and partly so I could clean the rest of each carpet he started cleaning!

Of course 'Renewals' sets insurance sales apart from all other ventures.

But I remember my first "Aha" moment in this business. Now you could say that my Aflac story began long before I ever started as an agent. It was July of 1999 when a drunk-driver ran my delivery van off the highway. My van hit a tree head on, and then I rolled down an embankment. I broke a vertebra in my back, could barely walk for 7 months…I lost my house, lost everything! (I didn't have Aflac then). But now fast forward to my "Aha" moment.

It was approximately 2010, possibly 2 to 3 years in the business. I remember getting a call one evening. I didn't recognize the number, and almost didn't answer it, but I did. For several minutes I had no idea who I was talking to on the other end of the phone…thinking that perhaps it was a 'wrong number'. I actually wanted to hang up, but something inside didn't let me. I 'finally' realized who she was. I had in fact never met this lady, but a year earlier, her husband had purchased the accident policy from me at a voluntary fire department. Well, he had just fallen off a ladder. He wasn't putting out a fire or anything, but was emptying the gutter at his house. A rung cracked, and he came crashing down on top of his kid's toy truck in the yard, bent in half, and had suffered a collapsed lung. (This is still weird to me) but I believe I was her first call she made from the intensive-care unit at Catholic Medical Center. She was like, "What do I do? What do I do?". (Literally, in the back of my mind I'm thinking "why are you calling me first lady?") but she was just in a weird place and totally not herself, hysterical, and in a crisis. (Apparently her husband had me saved under "A" as "Jonny-Aflac" on his phone, so she saw the number and just hit 'call'.) Again, in my head I'm wondering why I am her first lifeline, but I did my best to calm her down with, "Listen, don't worry. Everything's going to be okay. Don't even think about paperwork or claims stuff right now, I'll get that all later. For now, just stay by his side. He needs you right now." I think I said a little prayer with her to make her feel better.

Well fast-forward months later. I'm walking in the front door of the same town's police department for an open enrollment meeting. I didn't know that the lady who called me that night was the dispatcher there! When she saw me walk in, she literally ripped her headset off, ran around the counter, and hugged me, with literal tears in her eyes, and said, "Thank God you sold him that policy. We wouldn't have a house if you didn't. He's still not back to work yet."

Now it was a little embarrassing, all these tough cops there for my open enrollment meeting and this lady's hugging me with tears in her eyes, but honestly, I was stunned for the rest of the day. All I could think about was how bad it sucked when I lost my house, and how this lady didn't have to go through what I went through because I sold her husband a policy.

I was already experiencing a healthy 6-figure income, taking dream vacations around the world etc., but it wasn't until that day that I really contemplated what a difference we are making in the lives of our policy holders.

Now that's something I can get behind!

When you become an Aflac agent, you not only represent the #1 most recognized brand in America, a company I believe 11 years running voted the 'most ethical company in the US', but you 'personally' are making a HUGE difference in the lives of your policy holders…all while creating the lifestyle of your dreams.

Welcome to AFLAC!

For years, my book fans have been asking me if I was going to write another book, or another volume of "You Can Too". For the first year or two, that wasn't my plan at all, but as my system progressed, and the base of individuals and teams that I coached increased, and especially as the ever-changing marketplace evolved, it became harder and harder to shake the idea that a second volume was bubbling up inside me.

I am now a Regional Sales Coordinator, managing 7 districts of my own. I've FAME'd approximately 18 times, and personally recruited and coached countless agents to success they personally never imagined. But one thing is for sure… change is inevitable!

I have an entire page in one of my business journals with a now famous quote from Dan Amos: "With Change

Comes Opportunity!" -spoken at FOCUS (In either Georgia or Texas) 2015.

Some people fight change. I know Blockbuster did. Believe it or not, Netflix approached the video rental giant with a proposal to join forces and capture the home-entertainment industry. Unfortunately for Blockbuster, they insisted that they were in the 'brick & mortar rent home-movies business', rather than merely the 'home-entertainment' industry. They could have dominated the market! But, being resistant to change, they got run over, became obsolete, and in fact closed their last store in early 2014.

Encyclopedia Britannica was the first company to put an entire encyclopedia on CD-ROM…but their sales force insisted that that would hurt their door-to-door efforts selling encyclopedias! When's the last time you heard of anybody buying 36 hardbound volumes of encyclopedias in a world where you can just ask 'Alexa', or Google any question?

I live an hour from Logan Airport in Boston, Mass. When I was a kid, ½ the airplanes used to say 'TWA' on the side. What happened to Kodak, Howard Johnson's etc., etc.? The same thing…they resisted change instead of learning to capitalize on it.

Well, "You <still> Can Too" (or You Can Too II), is all about how to take a great thing, the best opportunity in America, and make it way better!

I'm going to show you not only how to increase your Aflac business, but numerous strategies to actually get employers to 'pay for' Aflac for every one of their employees, even how to add to your portfolio with other insurance carriers, and many, many other strategies that will help you build a dynasty of a customer base, build your renewals to levels you never thought possible, and create real lasting wealth that will outlive you by generations.

As fun as the initial ride has been, buckle up...the next ride gets even better!

# Immediate Results Using My "You Can Too" System

*"Jonny,*

*No question about it, your presentation at our May 13 Statewide meeting had an impact on the Associates producing 70 M0138s the 13 working days that followed.*

*Thank You!"*

—Mike Butler SSC North Carolina
(Aflac Hall of Fame)

FOR SOME (A LOT) of people, the simplicity of my "You Can Too" system has baffled them. I think others, (who very well may have been in the business since long before I got here) feel that such a simple approach negates either the validity of the brand, or at least limits the array of ways a seasoned Aflac agent can assist a small business owner. Hopefully, within a few short chapters of this book, you will be assured that my goal is to actually fortify every account we acquire with not only several lines of business, but also a slew of value-added products and services so that the business owner perceives us as an indispensable asset to their company's success.

However, like the Ricky Henderson analogy in my first book, "you can't steal first base!"

You may be an amazing gentleman...one who is a fantastic listener, driven with a goal and desire to devote your heart and soul toward raising a family, a desire to provide a lifestyle for your future bride that others envy. You may be a door opening, "please and thank you" kind of guy, that even has a soft spot for rescuing animals...perhaps 'exactly' what a girl dreams of as a 'probably-doesn't-exist' kind of fairy-tale husband. But if you never convince her to go on a 'first date', she'll never know that you could be that man of her dreams.

Similarly, you may contain a wealth of knowledge on everything from pre-tax payroll deductions, assisting with one-day-pay claims, to truly understanding all the details of major medical insurance, from co-pays to co-insurance... but without that "first date", that business will never know.

Now, can you imagine going to 10 small businesses, meeting 10 business owners, and booking 10 appointments in 30-60 minutes...one-day-a-week? I can. I can because I've done it countless times, and so have many of my agents.

It 'can't' be that easy, right?

Well, easy or hard, I will echo that it really is that simple.

My first 7 weeks full time with Aflac, I closed 21 accounts. In my first year, I was the #1 account opener in all of Aflac (out of 61,000 agents) writing 72 accounts in 11 months, (and I took 6 weeks vacation, and almost every Friday off). But when I was working, I was a machine, from 8:30 to 3:30, Monday through Thursday.

After just under a year as an associate, I became a DSC. My first year as a district, we wrote 123 accounts. In year 2 we wrote 151 accounts. And my third year as a DSC, we finished the #1 district in the company, writing 241 accounts. (In fact that year, I had 9 separate agents on my team that closed at least 20).

Now drive did have an awful lot to do with it, sure. My vision of what I was looking to accomplish certainly got me out of bed in the morning…absolutely. But still, it was the simplicity of my system that generated such immediate success.

DISCLAIMER: I'll remind you that I don't claim that my system is the 'only' way to do this business. And certainly, there are countless agents with very successful careers with Aflac that have never used my methods, or in fact retired long before I arrived on the scene. I have befriended countless agents and managers that have become very efficient appointment setters by using the phone. However, I will hold to my opinion that my system is the 'simplest & fastest' way to enjoy immediate success.

Remember, my wife Michelle and I had just joined our families, and we had 8 kids under our roof when I was just starting out…and my mortgage was over $5300/month! I can tell you honestly that we never missed a mortgage payment, thank God, but I can totally relate to you if you are absolutely living from one enrollment to the next, desperately trying to make ends meet and put food on the table. I needed one thing when I started, and that was constant cash flow, or else I would've been forced to pursue a different career path.

Every morning I started my day by pulling up 'my statements' and 'daily deposits' to see what I made the day before. Some days it was $200, some days it was $2000, but

I needed to see a deposit almost every single day. How did I do that? By getting almost every business to say yes to that 'first date'.

## The Science of the Opening Line

The 'opening line' of my system has been the single biggest game-changer for countless associates. But why does it work so effectively?

In my first book I taught the 'magic' opening line, but now let me go deeper and explain the psychology of why it works.

"Hey, how are you? I haven't had a chance to meet you yet. I'm Jonny the Aflac guy and I work with a bunch of your neighbors. I'm on the way to Boston today, but I think I'm back in this area one more time, I think next Thursday. Say…if I stop by can you give me 5 minutes with a brochure? You've seen the duck on TV right?"

"Of course."

"Great, what's your name?"

"Jason."

"Jason, good to meet you. Have a great day!"

BAM!

That 'exact' approach has netted my team over 1000 accounts.

But 'why' does it work? Allow me to explain.

During the 15 second 'conversation', what were the prospect's 'lines'?

"Of course." (or "yes" or "sure")

"Jason."

There is something magic that happens when you speak a positive affirmation. If you're a parent, you know that kids somehow are born knowing the word "No!". It's an immediate untrained response. But it takes more effort, like squatting in front of that toddler, making eye contact, and nodding your head as you softly say "Yeeessss" before they repeat it. But when they do, a positive endorphin fires in their brain, and they feel good about themselves. Now that prospect said "Yes" or "Of course" to the question beckoning a positive response, "You've seen the duck on TV right?". Again, unless they've lived in a cave without a TV, everyone's seen the duck, right?

And what was his second line? "Jason." What is everyone's favorite subject? Themselves right? And immediately after he said his name, I repeated it. Music to his ears...

So again, the prospect says "Yes", and then their name, I repeat their name, and I leave. Now the business owner has no idea why, but they like me a little bit. Actually, this is crazy, but it works!

I volunteered at Plymouth University in NH where 'sales' is actually something a student can major in. I partly want to impart big dreams without limitations on the next generation, but I also literally teach my 'system' to the kids. I have them roll-play my Aflac line, and then I change it up.

Listen to this,

"Hey, how are you? I'm Jonny the flower guy, and I deliver to a bunch of your neighbors, but haven't had a chance to meet you yet. Unfortunately I'm on the way to Boston right now, but I think I'm doing this route one more time next Thursday. Say... if I stop by next week and happen to catch you, can I show you a sample of my bouquets? You like the smell of flowers don't you?"

"Of course."

"Great, what's your name?"

"Jason."

"Jason, good to meet you. Have a great day!"

Now I think you'll admit that unless you're evil, you like the smell of fresh-cut flowers right? They have to say "Yes" or "Of course", and…their name.

You could be the 'Cookie Guy' and say, "You like the smell of fresh baked cookies don't you?" Who doesn't?

If you sold frozen steaks (like I used to), "You like great food don't you?".

Now are you living on borrowed time? Yes. But at least she's not surprised when I pull up in the car for that 'first date'. You can 'sell yourself' to that girl that you might be the man-of-her-dreams much better over a filet mignon and a glass of wine than you ever could've when you first introduced yourself. Same here.

Now next Thursday when you do pop back in, and make eye contact with that business owner again, a 're-memory' endorphin fires again, because the last time you made eye-contact, that business owner 'felt better' about themselves, even if only for a moment.

The next step we will revisit in a later chapter, but get 'On Base' hundreds of times using this method, and you'll propel yourself to an incredible career with Aflac, and the lifestyle that follows.

Hey, do you remember Tim from my first book? We did pick on him for having to take the insurance exam 6 times before finally passing. He even earned the nickname "6". But guess what his nickname "6" stands for now? To date he's the only agent I've ever known to get 6 M-0138s signed in a single day (the equivalent of 6 AOD calls in a day)! Tim was the first student of my system, and to this day is "Tim, the Aflac guy".

Keep this part simple. Rewind, play. Lather, rinse, repeat. Get real good at the opening line and everything else will happen from there.

# MMA fighter Johnny Burgess aims to set world record
## November 18, 2017
**Union Leader**

Mixed martial artist Johnny Burgess will attempt to accomplish one of his life's goals by setting a world record, while at the same time giving kids stricken with cancer a fighting chance of survival.
Burgess, the owner of Team Burgess MMA in Manchester and the principal for the Aflac Insurance agency in New Hampshire, intends to eclipse the Guinness Book of World Records mark of breaking 2,897 one-inch wooden boards with his hands in one hour. This record has stood since May 10, 2003. The attempt will be from 5:45 to 6:45 p.m. tonight prior to the start of Combat Zone 64 at the Downtown Radisson Hotel in the Queen City.

"Ten years ago, I wrote down 100 life goals, and this is one of them that I haven't crossed off the list yet. I plan to break 3,400 boards," he said.

Burgess and his wife, Michelle, who have a blended family of eight children, are coupling the attempt with a fundraiser for The Aflac Cancer and Blood Disorders Center at Children's Healthcare of Atlanta.

Burgess, 49, has been involved in martial arts since he opened his first karate studio at age 16 and was still in school.

"It's mostly mental," Burgess said of his training for tonight. "I've conditioned my hands over the years from doing traditional karate."

# NH man breaks world-record number of boards

<u>November 18, 2017</u>
**Union Leader**

Johnny Burgess, the owner of Team Burgess MMA, set a world record for most one-inch pine boards broken by hand in one hour at the Downtown Radisson Hotel in Manchester on Friday night.

Burgess broke 3,676 boards according to the official early tally, and will now be entered into the Guinness Book of World Records. The karate expert accomplished one of his lifetime goals prior to the start of the Combat Zone 64 card of pro and amateur MMA and amateur kickboxing action.

"The previous record was set in September and we just passed it by more than 400 boards," said Burgess, 49, afterward while soaking his bloodied and swollen hands in ice water. "Mentally, I never had any doubt that I could do this. The only question was if my hands could hold up, and luckily they did. When they finish all of the counting, I think the final official tally will be more than 3,700 boards."

The entire amount of the money raised through sponsorships and cash contributions, which will still be accepted, will be donated to the Aflac Cancer and Blood Disorders Center at Children's Healthcare of Atlanta.

"This took a lot of planning and it was a lot of work. Hopefully, we raise a lot of money to help the kids," said Burgess, who heads up the Aflac Insurance agencies in New Hampshire.

# Visualize Your '100'

On November 18th, 2017, at the Combat Zone event held at the Radisson Hotel in Manchester, NH, I literally "Smashed" the previous world record by breaking 3,676 1-inch pine boards with my bare fists in less than an hour.

What in the world would make/inspire me to attempt such an incredible endeavor? Well, 9 ½ years ago, when I started my Aflac career, I wrote down 100 very specific life goals that I intended to accomplish. Some people call it a 'bucket list'. I actually hate that. That makes it sound like something that you hope to do just before you die. I want to accomplish the things on my list while I am still very much alive! And thanks to this great Aflac opportunity. I've already crossed off dozens of items from my list. Some are relationship goals and personal, others are dream destinations. Some are desired accomplishments, others are net-worth monetary objectives.

If you honestly believed that nothing was impossible, and that you couldn't fail, what would your '100' look like?

For some reason, I wrote "dog sledding" as one goal. Guess what? I 'happened' to win a trip with Aflac to

Whistler Canada and there 'happened' to be one last minute opening on the dog sled run...and guess what? I crossed that one off!

I wrote "swim with dolphins". I just 'happened' to be in Atlantis, Bahamas...and I crossed that one off.

I had never seen the Grand Canyon, so that was on my list. Well I 'happened' to win an Aflac National Convention trip to Vegas. Guess what? Yup, my wife Michelle and I took a day road-trip to see the Canyon...and crossed off that one.

"Seeing Hawaii" was on my list, and I 'just happened' to win an Aflac trip to that destination as well... "Check!"

One of my favorites though was a restored relationship with my daughter Casey that for a while was estranged. Now, we're closer than ever... "Check!"

Come to think of it, one of my goals was "To pass on inspiration to all 8 kids". After publishing a book (now two), becoming a millionaire, breaking a world record, taking them on countless dream vacations...I think I can check that one off.

My list contained, "Break the board-breaking world record."—"Check!"

In the book "Success Principles", Jack Canfield (the author) recounts the story of Lou Holtz. Lou, a young married man with 2 kids, and a new home with the white-picket fence, had landed his dream job as an assistant football coach for a university in the south.

Well, as life would have it, he went from living the American Dream to a life of shattered dreams, as the head coach of the university got caught up in some kind of scandal, and the college ended up nixing their entire football program. Lou went from the mountaintop to the valley overnight, as he found himself unemployed. He had been 'all-in' on the life he had just created, pulling together every penny he had for the down payment on the American Dream home with the white picket fence.

He became a depressed mess...a miserable person to be around. Thankfully, his wife put a book in his hand, "The Magic of Thinking Big". That book challenged him to dream again, and even bigger. It also challenged him to write down a list of 100 goals that, if he knew he couldn't fail, would like to accomplish.

As an unemployed depressed mess, he had literally no business writing down goals like:

1.  Winning a National Championship

2.  Being Coach-of-the-Year in the NCAA

3.  Coaching for Notre Dame

4.  Having dinner in the White House

5.  Hitting a hole-in-one in golf

Although Lou may have had no business writing such audacious goals at the time, last I heard he had already accomplished 86 of his written life goals...including all 5 of those above!

Let me ask you a question. Do you think either you or I could ever convince Lou that his remaining 14 were too 'Far Out' to be legitimate goals? Heck No! Why? Because he's already crossed so many off his list. In fact, he's hit a hole-in-one not just once, but twice!

Now it's your turn. I hereby give you permission to think big...REALLY BIG! If you 'knew' you couldn't fail, what would you strive for?

Though I haven't tested the theory myself, I've heard that you can put 'fleas', like the kind you'd find on a dog, and put them in a mayonnaise or pickle jar. At first, you can not only see them jumping and banging off the lid, but you can actually hear them, kind of like the sound of popcorn in the microwave. Before long, the "ting-ting-ting" sound starts to slow down, and eventually stops altogether. What happened? Well the fleas inside the jar learn very quickly that jumping any higher than a certain point actually hurts, and they figure out just how high they can jump without it 'hurting'.

Ready to hear something crazy? If you ever-so-slowly untwist the lid off the jar, the fleas still won't jump out of the jar! Unfortunately they learned that jumping 'too high' hurts.

How unfortunate, but it illustrates perfectly what also happens to so many people. We all have big dreams when we're young. What happens? We strive for one, don't quite make it, it 'hurts', and we learn very quickly that jumping too high can hurt, and "I'm not going to do that again!"

Well it's time to take the lid off. You CAN dream big again! Getting knocked down isn't what makes or breaks a man…it's whether or not he gets back up.

The world needs you to get back up. Your family needs you to get back up again. People you haven't even met yet will be able to 'do life' better because they'll love and want to emulate your tenacity.

If you haven't started 'Your 100' yet, there's no better time than right now. Don't put it off! And just 'thinking' about them doesn't count. It's not real until you put it in ink.

It honestly doesn't matter if anybody else sees it; this is 'your' list. I would even caution you to be very selective who you share your list with.

Stay away from dream stealers!

I promise you, there are people who would love to talk you out of your list. Their reason for trying to drag your dreams back down from the clouds is that if you actually succeeded, they'd look bad, or inferior. It's SO sad. They honestly should come up with their own '100', but many never will.

Can you imagine if everybody you came across had their own '100' driving them? Everybody would spring out of bed every morning ready to conquer the world, driven by the pursuit of their own specific dreams. Indeed, the world would be a better place.

The interesting thing is that the first 20, 30, 40 maybe even 50 will come to you fairly easily. Some dreams that you've held since childhood might eagerly come back to mind. At first, most of the goals will be material…like exotic cars, dream destinations, homes etc., and other 'stuff'. But after so many of those, it starts to slow down, and now you start thinking beyond yourself. Now you start wondering, "How can I make this world a better place because I'm in it?" Now it's stuff like "Sponsoring 100 World Vision Kids" (actually one of mine), "Supporting a food ministry" etc. Then your list has truly come full circle.

So, one last time, I hereby give you permission to dream again. Think big…REALLY BIG! Start getting your '100' to paper, and treasure it.

Now the key is to look at your list very regularly. My method may seem a little far out to some, but most Saturdays I spend about 2 hours in my hot tub outside, visualizing 'My 100'. I start with an attitude of gratitude, thanking God for every one I've already crossed off. Then, in as much detail as I can muster, I visualize every one of the remaining goals on my list.

What's amazing is that when I broke the world record in November, the event happened 'exactly' as I had envisioned it literally hundreds of times over the last 9 years. I had been there countless times in my mind while in my hot tub.

Get crystal clear about what you want to accomplish.

I've done a ton of 'book-signings' across the country as I've spoken in various states at Kick-offs, National Training Days etc. I always sign the inside cover with "Think Big… REALLY BIG!" And "May God grant you the desires of your heart" -Psalm 37:4.

I believe with everything in me, that God is the one that plants those dreams in your heart, and He WILL help you get there!

# How The First Book Came To Be

PEOPLE HAVE ASKED ME how I ended up writing the book "You Can Too" in the first place. Let me share with you exactly how it came to be.

In the previous chapter, I shared with you my 'routine' of how most Saturdays I spend 2 hours in my hot tub visualizing 'my 100'.

Well, at the end of my rookie year with Aflac I finished as the #1 associate in the country, opening 72 accounts in 11 months. Then, just before my 1-year anniversary, I was promoted to DSC. As I began assembling my team here in southern New Hampshire, I basically just told them, "This is what I did…Do this/do that…This should work…"

In my first year as a DSC, 3 agents on my team were 'also' in the top 10 in opening new accounts. Suddenly, it wasn't just me being some Rockstar salesman, but it turned out that anybody who used my 'system' could experience the same results. Soon after, I was also invited to speak at my first Kick-off, in New York, and taught my system for the first time.

So, it was a Saturday like most others during my first year as a district manager, and I was in my hot tub...visualizing my 100. Suddenly, this overwhelming thought came into my mind, "Write a book about what you just did."

At first I thought I was just losing my mind, like maybe I just had some bad pizza the night before, but honestly I couldn't shake it! Today I honestly believe that it was God ordaining my steps, to ultimately give him the glory for it all, and I began to shift from my own success to helping others.

Now 'Publishing a Book' WAS is fact one of my 100, however I had no idea at the time when I wrote down that goal that I would ever write a book about Aflac. Remember, I wrote 'my 100' before finishing my rookie year as the #1 account opener in the country.

I literally couldn't shake it, so I climbed out of the hot tub and went into the house, walked over to the computer with a wet towel wrapped around me, and started typing (with the same finger I play piano with).

Over the course of the next 4 or 5 days, I completed the introduction and the first 2 chapters. The following Thursday was 'Stampede', an annual event where every coordinator in the eastern half of the United States gathered once a year. As a new DSC, this was to be my first. The event was to be held in Baltimore, Maryland.

Somehow in my soul, I knew (or felt impressed) that someway/somehow, I needed to get those first few chapters into the hands of Paul Amos, or "P-2" as they call him, grandson of the founder of this great company. (This was before he changed roles and left to take over operations for Aflac-Japan).

I remember that morning in the Manchester airport, asking my then Regional Manager Bill Henry, "Do you think Paul Amos will be there?"

He said, "He should be".

"Great" I answered, "I just wanted to meet him".

I didn't even tell Bill my plan that I intended to put my 'book' in Paul Amos' hand, honestly for fear that I thought he might try to talk me out of it.

Well, the plane landed, and we were eventually shuttled to the beautiful Marriott Hotel. I remember being amazed at just how many (literally hundreds) of managers there were arriving for the event.

I checked in at the front desk, got my room key, and with my rolling suitcase in tow, headed toward the elevator banks, and pressed the "up" button.

Now there must have been 6 or 8 elevators there. As the bell 'dinged', and the next available elevator door opened, I entered. Now you might not believe this, but guess who the only other guy in the elevator was? You guessed it...Paul Amos. (I had only seen him in pictures up to that point).

There I was, silently staring at the illuminated numbers going up, indicating our assent 12,13,14,15...

I believe my destination was the 28th floor. My heart started pounding. I was thinking to myself "This is really Freaking happening!".

I suddenly blurted out, "Paul Amos, I'm Jonny Burgess. I was the #1 account opener in the country last year. I think God told me to write a book. Here's the first couple chapters. Tell me what you think."

"Ding!" The elevator arrived at the 28th floor, I stepped out, and the door closed behind me. I can't explain what I was feeling, but I was thinking, "Wow, that just happened! I may be fired, but I did it!"

Well the next day, in between sessions, we finally had a 'break' of a couple hours before dinner. I couldn't wait to chill out in the hot tub for a while, and contemplate all that I had just learned and everyone I had met over the last day and a half. (By the way, I love hot tubs!)

There I was, in my swimsuit, towel around my neck, getting in the elevator to go down, and guess who (again) is the only other guy in the elevator? Paul Amos!

He told me, "Jonny, I read it, love it, and can't wait to see the rest of it", and he gave me the 'thumbs up' sign.

That was all I needed.

Over the next couple months, I wrote the rest of the book. (BTW...my wife later told me that almost every chapter was in a different font).

I accomplished my goal of completing it by 'Convention', which that year was a cruise to the Bahamas. On the ship, I handed a copy (very rough cut version in manila envelopes) to a few key people including Mike Chille, Ron Sanders, and...Paul Amos.

*I would also like to thank Jim Thompson (Aflac Hall of Fame) who also gave me very valuable feedback after proof-reading the first draft for me.*

Now I had no experience up to that point as to what an endeavor proof-reading and editing was going to be, but close to a year later, it finally hit the press...and to this day hundreds and hundreds of agents (and managers teaching my system) buy "You Can Too" at Barnes & Noble, Borders, or Amazon...or purchase the e-book version from Kindle or I-Tunes for their tablets and I-Pads.

Since then I've had the privilege to speak in I believe 21 states for either SSCs, RSCs, Kick-offs and trainings.

I am so thankful for what the Aflac opportunity has been able to provide for me and my family...and I feel that this is the way I can 'Give Back' so to speak, and pay it forward.

Now if you think that my bumping into Paul Amos (twice) among the hundreds of managers was sheer coincidence, I don't know what to tell you. But I know that it's evidence that when you get crystal clear about your vision and what you want to accomplish, then somehow things fall into place just the way they're supposed to.

# How Big is BIG?

HERE IN THE NORTHEAST, our Territory Vice President, Ken Meier, has a vision. His desire is to one day have 'every' single W-2 employee in the northeast, from West Virginia to the very top of Maine, have access to an Aflac cancer policy through pre-tax payroll deduction. They don't have to all buy it, but eventually he sees every company 'offering' it to every employee.

Now is that big of a vision a little far out? Well, remember who you're talking to here... I think it's a great vision. We certainly have a ways to go, but why not?!

Many reading this may not know the name Bill Rosenburg. Years ago, he was nothing but a man with a dream. He loaded a canteen food truck every morning and drove around to construction sites selling his coffee and pastries. He eventually opened his first 'brick and mortar' donut shop in 1948 in Quincy, Massachusetts. He had scraped together $1500 to invest, and borrowed $1000 more. His first shop, "Open Kettle" was a success, and in 1950 it was renamed "Dunkin' Donuts."

Bill Rosenburg had a vision too, a big one. He envisioned his shop, and the Dunkin' Donuts name, on every street corner in America. In 1955 he started multiplying, and his franchise concept eventually spread from coast to coast.

I may be partial, being a New Englander, but I think their coffee is the best, (and so are their croissant breakfast sandwiches). Almost ten years ago, I was very pleasantly surprised to be able to get a Dunkin's coffee in the Bahamas as our cruise ship docked for the day. I remember when in my prior life in food sales, I worked in Cleveland, Ohio for a week (probably around 2002), and it may have been quite a drive clear across town, but they had in fact just opened a Dunkin's in Cleveland.

With all my trips to Florida and Disney World, I can't help but notice how many Dunkin' Donuts are popping up all across the Sunshine State.

I was probably most surprised when I saw one in Spain!

Unfortunately, Mr. Rosenberg passed away not too long ago, but not before he saw his vision spread to over 37 countries! And guess what? There is a Dunkin' Donuts at virtually every street corner in America.

Now as good as his coffee is, I think Kenny's vision of a cancer policy (arguably our best product), even at no cost to the employer, available at every company…is an even nobler cause!

How big is your dream?

How much can you envision making a year with Aflac?

I always ask my interviews what they are looking to make a year. Both today, and what about 5 years from now, and 10 years from now?

It's sad that most people don't even have a number in their mind. Or if they do mutter a number, it's almost apologetic in case it was too high.

Whatever their answer, I always challenge them to think bigger.

Our Market Director shared at a recent training that he left the field when his renewals reached over $50,000/month! (Before he took a W-2 position with Aflac Corporate).

I hope that helps you start thinking a little bigger.

I heard of another coordinator in the northeast who 'retired' with renewals of $250,000/month!

Um, hello...that's a walk-away '7-figure' income, even if you don't get out of bed!

Now, you may not quite comprehend that big of a dream...yet. But I believe faith is like a muscle, and as you begin to have successes, you'll gradually allow your mind to push the limits.

I'll ask you one more time, "How big is your dream?"

# 'Milk Route'

Zig Ziglar once said that if you're not jumping out of bed in the morning to conquer the world, it's because your dreams are not big enough.

My dreams are pretty big, and I do in fact spring into action every morning, without needing an alarm.

But the more specific you are with your desired outcome, the more focused you'll be in getting there.

Let's look at what a 'milk route' of 100 accounts looks like...

Regardless how long it took to get there, let's picture getting out of bed and servicing a book-of-business comprised of 100 small accounts. Let's not even consider any large companies or employers being in the mix, let's simply say you have 100 small businesses, with let's say 3 to 25 employees, from hair salons to diners, from pizza shops to garages to pre-schools.

What if ½ of them had just 1 new hire/quarter. Simply, every 3 months, ½ of them employed a new dishwasher at the pizza shop, one new hairstylist at the salon, a new mechanic at the garage. What would that look like for you?

Well that's 50 new hires, and let's say we average $800 in AP per employee (about 2 policies per), maybe an accident and a dental.

Well that's $40,000 in premium every quarter.

X's 4 quarters = $160,000 AP, working very part time. Basically you're meeting 1 new employee/day, Monday through Thursday, with Fridays off.

Now that's $160,000/year just on new hires, in small accounts. Next, let's assume that without too much effort, we write another $40,000 throughout the year...picking up an occasional new account through a referral, open-enrollments (where some companies have you sit with 'every' employee once-a-year to review their benefits), and possibly an occasional invitation to an MLA enrollment. Nothing outrageous, but literally averaging another $400/year in each account...that's it. But that now brings you to a total of $200,000/year in AP.

Now remember, this is not your 'total' income, because you're still being paid renewals on all the business that's already on the books...this is just new business...additional income.

But on the $200,000 in AP (annual premium), let's assume a 35% commission, fair enough? (Dental, vision, and accident may be a little lower, cancer and critical-care is usually 40%, and life pays 50%, but let's just go with an 'average' of 35%).

That's $70,000/year working very part time...plus $7,000/year in Aflac stock! But more importantly, we're adding to our renewals, year after year. Let's take a look...

Again, accident being less and life being more, I'll take the liberty to use the cancer policy as the standard, which pays 7% renewals.

That's an 'increase' in your renewals of $14,000/year.

Now real life is…not everyone keeps their policies going forever. Some don't keep their Aflac when they leave an employer. Some age out of disability, some life policies term, some of our policy holders pass away. But let's use the national consistency rating of 76%. That means 76% of the business you write 'does' stay on the books and goes into renewal status. So your real increase in renewal income is $10,640/year. That's how much of a raise you are giving yourself, year after year. In 10 years, you've 'increased' your renewal income by $106,000/year! How many people (especially when working part-time about 10 hours/week) get a 'raise' of $10,000/year? Only in America, only with Aflac!

Not a bad business plan at all.

Remember, getting 'to' 100 accounts is not supposed to be a 20-year project. I opened 72 accounts my first year!

In my region, the focus is on making this a 5-year objective or less.

I'm still only 9+ years in the business, and let's just say I make several times that. This is very real.

Now for some, at this point you may very well have arrived. You may choose at this point to take a year off and tour this great country in an RV, from the Redwood Forest to Mt. Rushmore, to Niagara Falls to the Everglades.

Perhaps you can devote yourself to missions at this point.

One of my friends Jim Bergdoll is currently living out a boyhood dream, thanks to Aflac. With this opportunity, Jim and Evelyn were able to pay off their house entirely in just 9 years, then Jim retired with a comfortable 6-figure renewal income.

And now…Jim just became a police officer near Bangor, Maine! As a boy, he dreamed of wearing the badge, billy stick, the gun and the flashing blue lights. Well, he just literally went through the police academy, and became a cop!

Admittedly, I doubt he'll do it for long, because it's a real job where you have to punch a clock etc., and he's not doing it because he needs the money, but he's living the dream...literally. (By the way, Jim helped me a lot when I first got started, and a lot of my system is derived from how simple he taught me to keep things).

What will your life look like when that's you?

Perhaps, like me, yours dreams are way bigger than that. Let's look at what building your 'milk route' to 200 accounts will look like.

Again, let's say none of them are large dream accounts, and still just half of them have just one new hire/quarter. If you do the same math, that's $320,000/year AP, literally writing '2' new hires/day...still taking Fridays off. Let's assume the same $40,000/year with a couple referred new accounts (without really trying), MLAs, open enrollments etc.

Well that's $360,000/year AP. Again, using a 35% commission means a measly $126,000/year in new commissions, and $12,600/year in Aflac stock.

But what does that do to your renewals?

$360,000 X's 7% is $25,200/year increase. Again, to be realistic and use the national 76% national average consistency rating, your renewals are still growing by $19,152/year!

If you work a 200 account milk route for 10 years, you've increased your renewals by $191,520/year...plus your $126,000 in commissions.

Your 'part-time job' is netting you over $350,000/year!

Now this is NOT a pipe dream. In my region, Jeff White is our 'Milkman'…aka 'Aflac Idol' here in New Hampshire. (Ironically Jeff really was a milkman in his prior life). Well, most years Jeff writes in excess of $400,000/year. 'More' than the illustration we just spelled out. He became a member of the 'Million Dollar' club years ago.

I actually talk about Jeff in every interview. I use his story to sell the Aflac dream. When Jeff does show up for a meeting, he's sure to volunteer the fact that he just came from a facial or a massage. He's living it! Jeff hasn't knocked on a single door in years. He hasn't had to. But even he opened 4 new accounts in quarter 1 this year, simply from referrals that came to him.

And you probably (most certainly) will have a few big accounts. One agent David here in New Hampshire called on a small flat-roofed building years ago in Manchester, NH…having no idea that 'Easter Seals' had over 4000 employees, and that he would end up with a stop on his 'milk route' that gives him access to between 10 and 25 new hires every other Friday!

You'll land some of those accounts too.

I remember a couple years ago at Convention, Chris Cloniger, Aflac's money guy, displayed the top earners of Aflac nation. (Remember, Aflac is a full-disclosure publicly traded company, so everything is transparent).

Well here's what he displayed for the top earners in Aflac :

Top 1-50…………$1,250,000 average income
# 51-100…………$ 619,000
# 100-200…………$400,000
# 200-500…………$259,000

The top 500 (not the top 10, or any upper level management, but level 01 associates) had a combined average income of $422,000!

It's time to realize that this opportunity is real, and if you're not thinking big, it's time to.

Treat this Aflac opportunity as a business, not a job.

If becoming an Aflac agent cost $300,000 (like it is to buy even a small Dunkin' Donuts franchise) how hard would you work? And would you give up or get discouraged after having a 'bad day'?

And allow me to actually challenge your 'bad day' outlook. Did you get a lot of "Nos" today? Did a big enrollment cancel? I don't mean to sound unsympathetic... but that's 'not' a bad day. Sometimes it takes a time or 2 walking through the pediatric ward of the Aflac Cancer Center to realize that your 'bad day' is not so bad after all.

When you're a part of a child fighting for their life, and you get really bad news, or an unfavorable diagnosis...'that' just might be a bad day.

But really, the kids fighting for their lives are often the ones with the biggest smiles on their faces.

My wife Michelle served proudly as our Market's cancer ambassador for 4 years.

To brag on her just a little, she doubled the donations given from our Market to the Cancer Center during her tenure.

But the hard part of her position was actually getting to know the children (and their families) fighting that dreaded disease. The ironic part is that they actually did have 'bad days', yet they were in fact the ones with the infectious smiles. (I think that's why I love the Rachel Platten video of "Fight Song" now more than ever).

Anyway, (as I swallow back a lump in my throat), let's put bad days in perspective, and all your 'bad day' means is that you got a few "Nos" out of the way, on the way to building the lifestyle of your dreams.

By the way, at any part in your career, you can employ current Aflac agents to service your accounts for you. You can literally 'armchair quarterback' your way to even more success. Of course there's a split, but maybe you can be on the golf course a couple extra days each week.

The important part is that you take time to contemplate, and then visualize, your eventual 'final destination' in this business.

Let me say one more time, think big… REAL BIG!

# One Account at a Time 5 (4)-Minutes with That Business Owner

But how do you get to be 'The Milkman'?

The same way you eat an elephant…one bite at a time!

One account at a time. One door knock, one employer presentation, one employee presentation, one AOD call… all lead to an additional stop on the 'milk-route'.

Here's where I want to update my system and get you to appreciate the infamous 5-minute ER, and literally close 9 out of 10 ERs, and leave with a scheduled enrollment.

So you're popping your head back into that business that a week ago said "Yes" to the duck question. Now when you lock gazes, they may very well make the "Aflac!" noise again, and they will likely remember you from the week before. That re-memory endorphin fires again, reminding them that they 'like you a little bit'.

Remember, we very well may have simply told them we'd be stopping by, without a set appointment time necessarily, so we have to re-sell why we are there immediately. They're running a business don't forget, so don't expect to just walk in and have them immediately put their activities of the day on hold simply because you arrived. They're way too busy to listen to some boring hour-long sales presentation, and will do whatever necessary to get rid of you if they perceive that that's what you are after. But we can beat them to the punch by saying, "Hey, how are you? I'm Jonny from Aflac. I met you last week and told you I'd try to stop by when I was back in town. Unfortunately, I am on the way to Boston again this afternoon, but do you have time for that quick 5-minute version?"

We popped in unannounced, and asked (expected) to be able to give them our spiel, but 'before' they had a chance to tell us that they were too busy, we beat them to the punch. 'We' are actually the ones that are in high demand, extremely busy, and pressed for time…but to make good on our promise last week that we'd try to stop by, here we are.

Now, more than anything at this point, I hope they ask me one question…"Is it really 5 minutes Jonny?"

I look them right in the eye and say "Yes Ma'am/Yes sir, I bet I can do it in 4!"

At this point, the curiosity absolutely kills them, even if they were hoping it didn't. The #1 brand in America just walked in and said he can explain it in 4 minutes…"I gotta see this" is exactly what they're thinking.

Now I am going to show you exactly how literally 9 out of 10 times, 4 minutes later, I stand up with an enrollment scheduled in my datebook.

Don't hesitate, don't stall, don't small-talk…go right into it.

"Have you ever had Aflac here before?"

"No."

"Okay, but you've seen the duck on TV right?"

"Of course."

"Okay, we're not health insurance. Health insurance is important, but as you know it costs hundreds of dollars/month, goes up every year, and pays everybody 'but' you... hospitals, x-rays, doctors, nurses, etc. Aflac's totally different. If you can get Aflac at work like this, most of our policies are between $5 and $10/week, and we've never raised our rates on anybody since 1955. Nobody else can say that. But we send money to you, or to your employees, for every reason they came to work this morning...to pay the rent, mortgage, light bill, groceries, car payment, if something happened. What if they ever got hurt or sick?"

"We have several policies, but this one's our most popular. In fact I believe it's the most prescribed insurance policy in America." (Pulling out an accident brochure, and spinning it around to face the employer).

"If you've ever seen any of our commercials, where one guy has his leg up in a cast, and over here the duck's mailing out bills and ordering Chinese food...that's this one. It's the 'get hurt doing anything plan'. If you get hurt doing anything, on or off the job, 24/7, and have to go to a doctor, dentist, emergency room, chiropractor, hospital, walk-in clinic...or get ambulanced in, because you got hurt doing 'anything', we're going to send you money. At least $120 just for being looked at. It's kind of like a 1-day income replacement. We figure your employee could have been here at work making money, but instead they're in a waiting room waiting for an x-ray, chiropractor, or stitches. There's no fine print, (except maybe if you're committing a crime)..."

"And the easiest claim in the world is an Aflac claim. It's only 1 page, and I'm going to fill it out for you. Just tell me the address you want your check sent to, and on one line what happened, 'I stubbed my toe, sprained my ankle, chipped my tooth, poison ivy, sunburn'...whatever your 'accident' was, and you've got money in 4 days, or you can even sign up for 'One-Day-Pay', and get a direct deposit in under 24 hours!"

Now here's one step I started implementing years ago. I actually hold up a real claim form. A picture's worth 1000 words. Here we are blowing them away with the 'That was easy' claims process. As I say "the address you want your check sent to" I am drawing a circle around the top half of the claim form with my finger, and then point to where we indicate how the injury occurred.

"This is my wife's claim. Her finger got slammed in my grandson's toy box, and was all swollen and didn't look right. One sentence from her doctor stating 'Michelle hurt her finger on a toy box', and hours later we received a direct deposit for $220. Literally the easiest claim in the world."

# ACCIDENTAL INJURY CLAIM FORM

Failure to complete this form in its entirety may result in a delay in processing this claim.

☐ Complete Policyholder/Patient information and sign your claim form.

☐ Prior to mailing physician complete Section B (Physician Statement) and sign the order form or if hospitalized and/or confined to an hospital upon outpatient visit, please send a copy of your hospital UB showing charges and the number of days you were confined. Therefore claims related directly have your treatment monitored by recording a claim complete bill or individual UB.

☐ If you are filing for disability, please complete the initial Disability Claim Form (DXX24) as well. Forms are available on our web site at afiac.com.

☐ All bills should include the diagnosis, service rendered, and actual charges for the service.

## Policyholder Information
(Please print.)

Policy Number

First Name: _Jasmine_    Initial    Last Name: _Burgess_

Mailing Address: _____

City: _Boston_    State: _NH_    Zip: _0310_

Check box if this is a new permanent address ☐

Social Security Number    Phone Number: (603) ___

## Patient Information
(Please print.)

First Name: _Michelle_    Initial    Last Name: _Burgess_

Relationship:
☐ Primary Policyholder  ☒ Spouse    Sex: ☐ Male  ☒ Female    Patient Birth Date: _____

☐ Dependent Child  ☐ Check here if dependent child is a full-time student. (If over the age 19, please provide school name and contact information.)

Please answer the following questions. The claim cannot be processed until all necessary information is provided.

Date of accident: _2/6/16_    Describe how the accident occurred: _Fall_

_Left arm / Head / Chest_    _Leg_    _Bumped on a bench_

Location of the accident?  ☐ On the Job  ☒ Off the Job  ☐ Other (please describe): _____

Was the patient the driver in a motor vehicle accident?  ☐ Yes (Attach the police report)  ☒ No

☐ If the patient sought treatment (*60 / *100) or once mile from his/her residence and required lodging for patient's relative while the patient was confined to hospital then submit the latest receipts. Please check your policy to verify the mileage your policy covers.

Any person who knowingly and with intent to defraud any insurance company or other person files an application for insurance or statement of claim containing any materially false information or conceals for the purpose of misleading, information concerning any fact material thereto commits a fraudulent insurance act, which is a crime, and subjects such person to criminal and civil penalties.

CLAIMANT SIGNATURE    FAMILY RELATIONSHIP, IF NOT POLICYHOLDER    DATE: _7/17/16_

American Family Life Assurance Company of Columbia (Aflac)
Attention: Claims Department • Worldwide Headquarters • 1932 Wynnton Road • Columbus, GA 31993
For information or help filing your claim, please call toll-free 1-800-99-AFLAC (1-800-992-3522) or visit our Web site at aflac.com
Toll-free fax number 1-877-44-AFLAC (1-877-443-5222)

SXXXX    Page 1 of 2    XXX

Now to really nail it, I try to give an actual claim story that relates to their industry, such as "You guys have a lot of sharp knives in the kitchen, and some pretty hot ovens. I had a guy in a pizza shop in Methuen roll the pizza cutter right up the length of his hand once during a lunch rush. He spent the rest of the day with a bloody towel in the emergency room waiting for stitches, when he should have been in the restaurant making money. Well we gave him a $775 'laceration benefit', based on the length of his cut, to make up for the work he missed." And to really involve the prospective business owner, be sure to act out the motions of both the pizza guy slicing his hand with the roller, as well as acting out holding a bloody towel over his hand.

If you are just starting out and don't have your own claim stories to use yet, talk to your DSC and use theirs'. I'm sure they have a ton of claim stories they'd be happy to share with you. Or, use mine, from both this book and my first one. Remember, 'We' are Aflac.

So far I've given them a personal claim story, gone over the super EZ claims process, and given them an industry-specific claim story. Now for the naked sunburn story... 'every time'!

"Now when I say 'no fine print', I really mean it. We had a firefighter on his honeymoon (probably a couple umbrella drinks in) whose claim said 'Fell asleep naked, face up, on the beach', and he got something like $1500 for a sunburn!" If they don't at least chuckle at that, they must not have a pulse.

Finally, we slam it with a BIG claim. "But 'this' is really why you have Aflac. This poor guy didn't break his finger like my wife did...he broke his femur. I don't know what all these codes mean, but I know 'compound fracture' means his bone was sticking through his jeans. He had ambulance rides, MRIs, surgery, overnight stays, rehab… but while he was in the hospital, his sister helped us get all the documentation we needed, so by the time he got home, there was already over $20,000 in his mailbox! Now none of that went to the hospital. That paid his rent for a couple months, the light bill, still able to make his car payment. He's got kids, but this kept food on the table, and they still had heat. Now obviously a femur is worth more than a finger, but he could just focus on healing rather than just trying to get back to work too soon." It's critical you have a claim summary in front of you that you can point to, just be sure to black out the person's name and any personal information.

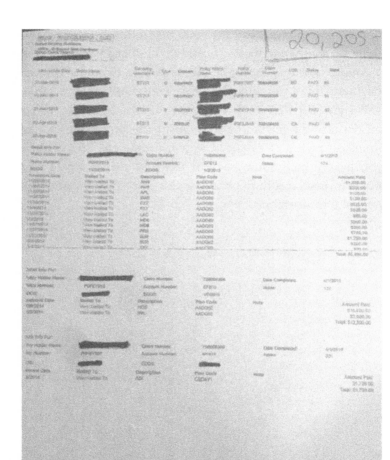

20,205

"And this even comes with life insurance of $40,000 should you ever die in a bad accident, God forbid."

"Now anybody in America can get this policy. If I'm at your kitchen table, this same coverage for your family is about $88/month. But if you can get it at work, it's usually between 5 and 10 dollars/week. Because you are a restaurant here in New Hampshire, you get one of the lowest rates in the country. I believe it's $7.10/week, and like a dollar-something to add a spouse…Any questions?"

Employer, "No not really, it sounds pretty amazing actually."

Don't hesitate…keep talking.

"We do have other policies too like maternity, dental, and vision, and they can get whatever they want, but this one here is the one that everyone gets" (holding up the accident brochure).

"The next step is…explaining this to your employees, just like I did with you, and it's been just under 4 minutes right? Just like I promised." (And I literally point to my watch). "I bring a little talking duck, so it's a little more fun, but it's really the same thing."

"What's the best time to get 'most' of your employees together for like 5 minutes, explain how this works, and send them right back to work, and see what kind of response we get?" While saying 'get them together' my hands almost come together like squeezing a small beach ball. Then I turn my hands over, and make a palms-out pushing motion as I say 'and get them right back to work'.

Now I just asked them a question, but I 'always' give a recommendation that I 'know' is not only the best time, but probably the 'only' time that might work for that particular industry.

"Probably nap time, when the kids are sleeping?" if it's a daycare. (Believe me, that's the 'only' time you want to enroll a daycare!)

"Probably first thing in the morning before the guys hit the road?" if it's a landscaping company. (Think about it, any other time of the day, the workers are spread clear across the state mowing lawns).

Or, "Probably around 2:30 between the lunch and dinner rush before it gets too busy?" if it's a pizza shop. (Again, having enrolled dozens of pizza shops, that's not only the best time, it's probably the only time that it's not too busy, but likely has both shifts coming and going, and there at the same time).

At this point, you not only make sense, but appear to understand their particular industry. It's funny, but they 'do' know their lines, "Yeah, that probably would be the best time."

Now at this point, I am about to add a simple 'linguistic body language' maneuver that works wonders…I ask for 'their' pen.

Actually, at about 3 minutes into my pitch, if I actually have my pen in sight, I subtly move my brochure on top of it. Now, once they agreed what the 'best time' would be, I go through the motion of patting my shirt and pants pockets, and say, "Can I borrow your pen?"

They 'always' hand me their pen, and that psychological effect of them involving themselves in closing the sale literally seals the deal.

I immediately open my datebook, accept their pen, and open to the month-at-a-glance page. It's an absolutely full mess of chicken scratch of blocked off days that he or she can visibly see, giving confirmation to them that I am in fact a super busy guy.

Now I fully understand that a lot of you reading this book are 'millennials', or close to it. I totally get that the next 2 generations after mine have gone 'paperless', and you probably have the rest of your year's schedule systematically programmed into your smart phone, and in fact by the time you finish reading this chapter, some alarm is likely to go off reminding you of an appointment later today. However, that does 'nothing' for you as a visual aid like an incredibly full datebook page does when it comes to credibility.

To get the point across, take a look at a literal page from my datebook. Would you believe I was a pretty busy guy if I opened it up in front of you?

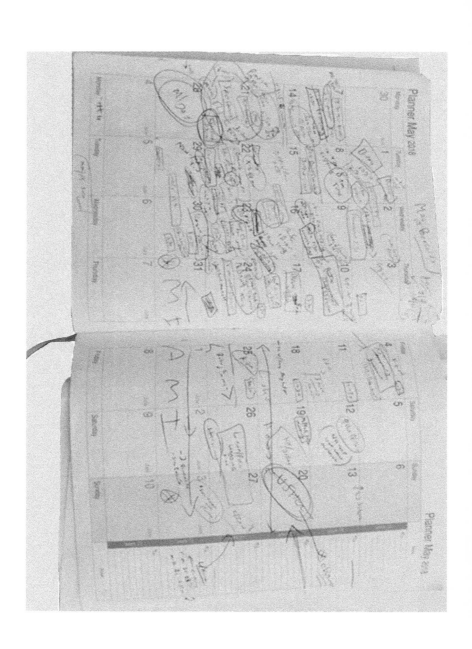

Now you may not be able to even read a lot of it. Honestly, neither can I sometimes. Thankfully my administrator Allie has a gift of translating my scribble so that many times she can help me figure out what I wrote down, (I'm serious!).

But please, for just a moment, put yourself in that business owner's shoes. Again, when they see my datebook, are they going to see me as a busy guy? Absolutely!

Letting a potential client know that I am in absolute demand is critical. Like I wrote in my first book, they want to know that 'everybody's doing it'. They want whatever you've got.

Now just imagine for a moment that you are pulling up to your dentist's office for a scheduled filling. You're pretty sure you're at the correct address, but you walk in, a little confused to say the least. The lights are on, and the door was unlocked, but the place is like a ghost town. There were no other cars outside (except for a beat up pick-up truck in the back corner). As you enter, there's not another soul in the lobby, but there in the back, you see a guy in a white coat with a drill in his hand, that says, "Come on back." Ummm…I might make some excuse why all of the sudden I need to reschedule my filling!

Not that I want to wait an unreasonable amount of time, but I want to see a waiting room full of apparently happy long-time patients sitting around the perimeter of the waiting room, and a shiny black BMW out front that assumedly belongs to the dentist.

Does your datebook make you look like that successful dentist? It needs to!

Okay, our business owner prospect has not only handed us his or her pen, but agreed to the best time of the day to address the employees. I just allowed him to close himself.

Now I open my extremely busy datebook, and I am about to ask him what's called a "Yes/Yes" question. I always say, "Okay, I'm booked the rest of this month", (As I turn the April page over to glance at May), "but the second week of May in the morning I could do either Tuesday or Wednesday…any preference?"

At that 'exact moment' I 'click' the pen he just handed me (or take off the cap) and look the business owner in the eyes, waiting for him to pick which day would work better for him, as I hover the pen over the Tuesday and Wednesday squares.

I remember laughing to myself when my daughter Cady used my own psychology on me. She'd ask, "Hey dad, can you bring me to Megan's after school, or should I ask her dad for a ride?" Notice, she never asked, "Hey dad, can I go to Megan's after school?" Of course not, that way she was asking a question which had 2 possible outcomes, a yes or a no. That's 50/50 odds, and that wasn't good enough for her. The way she asked was in the form of a "Yes/Yes" question, but either way she got to go to her best friend's house after school! I had to laugh, because I taught it to her, so I think I always said yes.

So do I care if the business owner picks Tuesday or Wednesday? Heck no, either way we just booked an enrollment!

"Um, Tuesday I guess."

Now I write 'ABC Landscaping' in the Tuesday square, hand him back his pen, shut my datebook, and start to stand up.

You might think that we just directed that business owner to do exactly what we wanted. You're right, we did.

But remember, the #1 brand in America just sat down, ran an entire meeting, impressed the owner, humored and entertained him a little bit, and got to the bottom line…in as little as 3 ½ minutes!

You certainly didn't waste any of that employer's time.

Also, take note that in my wording I mentioned, "And let's see what kind of response we get…" It's almost like I'm going to 'poll' his employees. Without this comment, human nature might just have the owner offer to 'poll' the employees himself, which most often is the kiss-of-death. Again, we beat him to the punch!

If you need to make a lot of money fast, master what I've just laid out for you. From the claim stories, to the full datebook, to the "Yes/Yes" question, to using 'their' pen.

Even before I had mastered my entire system, I closed 21 accounts in my first 7 weeks full-time with Aflac. To this day many of those very first accounts continue to be very profitable stops on my 'milk route', where new hires are written every year, and many have flourished into huge opportunities where I now have 5, 6, even 8 lines of business. In many of these accounts I've since assisted the owners in finding strategic ways to structure their health insurance…many times resulting in a situation where every new hire I meet with actually has a $25/week 'allowance' to go shopping for Aflac. Often times that's enough for an accident, sickness, dental, vision, cancer, and a small term-life policy! (I'll get to this in a later chapter).

But I originally closed them at a rapid fire pace using my very simple 5 (or 4) minute employer presentation!

Visualize your outcome! Imagine running 10 of these 4-minute employer presentations, and closing 5 (or 6 or 8) of them. I've done it so many times I've lost count. Sometimes, especially as you hone your skills, you'll close 10. That's the fastest way to build up lots of stops on your 'milk route'.

# Shelf Space

I KNOW A FEW people who've owned bread routes, including my father-in-law. It's a rewarding business, but is also a very demanding work load, not to mention a schedule that often starts at 2am! However, what I've always heard them say is that when it's say 11:00am, or noonish when the finished their route, if they had any energy left at all, they were always on the lookout for a new convenience or corner store that would allow them a tiny amount of 'shelf space'. It may be a mere 2-foot shelf on a lower level, but once you are awarded that little piece of real estate, you can build from there.

With Memorial Day and July 4th coming, you might place some red, white, and blue frosting cupcakes on the shelf. Right before Thanksgiving you might put out pumpkin pies. You'll probably display some sugar cookies around Christmas, something green prior to St. Patty's Day, and for sure some kind of cake resembling a football leading up to Superbowl Sunday.

As sales increase, you may very well be rewarded with even more 'shelf space'.

Treat your Aflac 'milk route' the same way.

Very seldom will a store award you the entire length of the 2 top shelves, though occasionally they may. But go get a ton of 'shelf space' opportunities, then we can expand our business from there.

The more you understand things such as psychology and NBL (neuro-linguistic body language), the better you'll perform out there. As simple as my 4-minute presentation may seem from the surface, there are countless angles from which we are appealing to our prospect, much of it subliminally.

I've done considerable research into various modes of psychology and human behavior...from birth order believe it or not, to the mentality of the baby boomers vs. Generation X and the millennials. I've read volumes on "The 5 Love Languages" (which I highly recommend, especially if you are married). I took a weekend course with the Worley-ID Profile, studied "Personality Plus", and "How to Win Friends and Influence People".

I've also studied the 'birds' in detail.

If you've recently attended Sales School (recently renamed 'Flight School'), you've been introduced to the birds. There are 4 types of people out there:

1. The Parrot-who always wants to have fun, and always enjoys a good story

2. The Eagle-(the other extravert)-who appreciates bottom line thinking, without a lot of fluff

3. The Dove-who is the epitome of a peacemaker/peacekeeper

4. The Owl-who is the ultra-organized detailed kind of person

If you've read my first book, you're probably not surprised to hear that I am an Eagle/Parrot. I'm very serious about getting things accomplished, in the shortest amount of time, but you can be darned sure that I am going to have a good time doing it!

Well the beauty of the 4-minute presentation is that you actually appeal to all 4 bird types at once.

For starters, the mere fact that you completed the task in under 5 minutes 'already' appealed to the eagle. No one could say you wasted their time.

A major theme in my first book is 'stories sell'. From the naked sunburn guy to any other claim story you kind of 'act out' appeals to the parrot big time.

The fact that the broken femur guy got $20,000 right away, and his kids are all still eating and the heat's still on won over the dove.

And even the owl is usually satisfied realizing that a broken pinkie may be worth $220 while a femur sticking out might get you 20-grand, on a sliding scale…the worse your injury the bigger the claim check…and "Because you're a pizza shop, it's only $7.10/week".

Now of course there are exceptions and extremes to everything, but in short you've accomplished what you set out to do…you've mastered a presentation that appeals to virtually everybody out there.

Get good at the little things, at the same time keep your vision big, and you'll be able to experience success at a level you've probably never imagined.

One quick story to demonstrate just how effective the 4-minute presentation is…

I had 'just' become a Regional Sales Coordinator. One agent that was now tracking to me was Cheryl. She had been in the business for 2 years or so, had had some initial success, but as of late had become extremely discouraged. She was about to quit, but thankfully her husband Ron made her reach out to me before pulling the plug. (Her husband had heard me speak at 'Kick-off' the year before. Ron is not an agent himself, but that particular year, spouses had been invited to the business session).

Hesitantly, Cheryl called me and said, "Jonny, I'm sorry to bother you, but my husband made me call you. I'm thinking this just isn't working out. I just ran 4 employee presentations, and not a single person signed up."

That had never happened to me, so I said, "I'll be right there".

We met at a local Dunkin' Donuts, and I asked her to share with me exactly what she was saying out there.

She proceeded to give me her employer presentation. She immediately handed me a laminated price sheet, detailing 11 products, and started explaining how to do pre-tax payroll deductions, (seriously).

Her DSC (at the time) honestly had checked out. His heart wasn't 'in it' to manage, and really had earned the right to kick it back a notch...already having a 6-figure renewal income, but this struggling agent needed more assistance than he was able to give.

Well about 10 seconds into it I said, "Okay, stop, stop... we've got to dial this thing way back".

The one thing Cheryl could do was book appointments, (ironically on the phone). She agreed that that was her strength, so we put together a plan of action. She would book a few appointments for the next week and I would run them for her.

I met her at the very first appointment, scheduled for a 10am presentation to the owner of a hair salon in Nashua, NH.

We walked in together, and the receptionist very promptly went out back to retrieve the owner.

When the owner emerged, she began to apologize, "Oh I'm sorry, I didn't realize that this was insurance. Sorry to waste your time, but I have a guy that takes care of all that for me."

Later that afternoon, Cheryl confided in me that when the owner uttered those words, her shoulders dropped a couple inches, and she thought to herself, "Great, another one of those", and "I can't believe I wasted Jonny's time like that".

Thankfully I was there, and I stepped in. I said, "Oh, I don't think you understand what this is. This doesn't replace anything you already have in place. In fact, if you already have health insurance, this works even better. We're already here anyway, can I give you the quick 3-minute version?"

She said, "Okay, since you're here, I'll take the 3-minute version."

With all the earnestness I possess, I'll tell you that about a minute and fifteen seconds into it, she said, "Oh, I had no idea. Can I get this for myself?"

I had gotten as far as the intro and the "Aflac's totally different", and a 1-page visual of a real claim... and her eyes got an inch wider, and I had her. She even said, "My husband's self-employed too, can he get this?"

I hadn't even gotten to the naked sunburn yet!

About 45 minutes later, Cheryl and I were on the way to McDonald's to transmit the business. (This is before we had 'hot-spots'). We had already enrolled the owner as well as the other 3 hair stylists in the salon. Most bought the accident and the sickness plans. We left with instructions for Cheryl to go back and enroll the remaining girls who were off that day. She did go back, and enrolled them too!

Cheryl's head was spinning to be sure, but she learned a valuable lesson that day.

Now if I had even attempted a big dissertation about the value of supplemental insurance, we would have been shown the door. But instead, we kept it simple, and enrolled the entire salon.

One more stop on the 'milk route'!

# Using the 5 (4)-Minute Pitch to Enroll New Hires

ONE OTHER WAY TO utilize the '5-minute' presentation is when you need to enroll new hires, in less than favorable enrollment conditions.

In a perfect world, the employees are sitting around a table in a break room, and the boss has already provided coffee and donuts for the occasion…"Aflac's Coming in!"

Later, with pre-tax, open enrollment, and 'guaranteed-issue' strategies, the perfect table has been set. But other times, you need to 'create something out of nothing'.

One of my accounts wasn't especially proactive rounding up the new hires for me, but they did at least allow me access to the floor.

I simply asked the HR for the names of the benefit-eligible new hires. I'd put the list in alphabetical order, and walk around the garage, office, and sales floor with my 'clipboard'. As I came across an unfamiliar face, I'd introduce myself, "Hey, I'm Jonny. I don't think I've had a chance to meet you yet. What's your name?"

They'd seem pleased to meet me, whoever I was…and they'd utter their name. Magically, I'd find their name on my list.

"You must not have been here last year. I do a lot of the benefits for the dealership here. Did they mention some of the benefits you're eligible for?"

At this point, part of the magic is acting like this conversation is supposed to be happening. You may get a few different responses. Some will assume that this is business as usual, and that they are expected to give you their attention. Others may say, "Oh, I told the office that I was all set with insurance".

If there's any resistance, I apply the reverse psychology, go along with it, and pretend to accept their disinterest.

"That's fine, I don't care whether you get anything or not, but I'm supposed to explain what's available to you. If you want, I can give you the quick 2-minute version, and then you can just sign something saying that I did a fantastic job explaining it, but you just don't need it this year. Fair enough?" And be sure to say all that with a smile.

Almost always, if you say it with a smile, they'll (even if it's begrudgingly) say, "Okay, I'll take the 2-minute version".

Don't hesitate…go right into it.

"Aflac's not health insurance. Health insurance is important, but as you know, it costs hundreds of dollars/month, goes up every year, and they pay everybody 'but' you… doctors, hospitals, nurses, x-rays etc. Aflac's totally different. If you can get it at work, most of our policies are between $5 and $10/week, and we haven't raised our rates on anybody since 1955." (Hold up the accident brochure). "We have dental, vision, disability, life…but this is the one everyone here has. It's the Aflac get-hurt-doing-anything-plan. "

"If you get hurt doing 'anything', on or off the job, 24/7, and have to go to a doctor, chiropractor, hospital, ER, walk-in clinic…anywhere, the first thing we're going to do is give you $120 just for being looked at. We figure you could've been here at work making money, but instead your sitting in a waiting room for hours, not making money, waiting for a chiropractor, x-ray, or stitch."

"And the easiest claim in the world is an Aflac claim. It's only 1 page, and I can fill it out for you. Just tell me the address you want your check mailed to, and on one line what happened…"I stubbed my toe, sprained my ankle, chipped a tooth, poison ivy, sunburn"…whatever, and you've got money within 4 days, or you can even sign up for 1-day-pay direct deposit".

"This is my wife's claim. She got $220 for getting her finger slammed in a toybox" (holding up the 1-page claim form), "and this poor guy got $20,000 because he broke his femur in a car accident", (and hold up a large claim summary).

"And it even comes with $40,000 life insurance if you ever died in a bad accident, God forbid."

"This is the most prescribed insurance policy in America. I think 65 million are covered under it already. If I'm at your kitchen table, it's probably around $88/month, but if you can get it at work, it's usually 5 to 10 dollars/week. This dealership actually has the 3rd lowest rate in the country, it's $6.10/week".

I hand him the pen, and 'click' it.

"Okay, just sign here saying you don't want it." (I already have a pre-filled PDA with his name on it, which becomes another powerful psychological tool).

I literally have my agents practice getting to the 'pen click' portion between 60 and 75 seconds.

The 'I don't care' backwards psychology works. I can't tell you how many times people have pulled back their hand, refusing to touch the pen, and said, "Wait a minute. I actually had no idea. I might actually be interested. How much did you say that was?"

A few will sign it, but many will buy it.

Just have fun with it. Act like you don't care, and play the game. Countless times they'll even say, "What else you got?"

Just this past week, 2 of my agents Tim and Brock implemented this exact strategy for a chain of Dunkin' Donuts. At first they sat like the 'leper-in-the-lunchroom', but thankfully they got pro-active enough to corral the manager and say, "Listen, I don't care if they get anything, but they're supposed to sit with us, just for a minute, and sign something saying they're all set." One-by-one they came, and Tim and Brock went 8-for-8 at the first location. By starting with, "I don't care if you get anything" and "This is not health insurance", their guards came down, and they enrolled. And most bought both an accident and a life policy!" Over the course of the next 2 weeks they maintained close to a 75% closing ratio, sitting mostly with employees that were 'all set'.

# More on Building
# That Milk Route

LET'S GET BACK TO adding 'shelf space' to our route.

Perhaps you have a referral. Some referrals are treasures, and the table's been set ahead of time, and the referred prospect is in fact 'expecting' you to stop by, and they welcome you with open arms.

Other times the 'lead' you receive isn't exactly blazing hot, but it's a name, and it's a place to start.

I'm now going to introduce you to the "1-11".

Going back to my first book, let's review how we obtained that referral.

In my opinion, the absolute best time to get a referral is right after an enrollment. There's electricity in the air, the employees are buzzing, and that business owner is impressed with your performance, and he can tell his employees are happy.

Now, 'just' before leaving, almost as a last-minute afterthought, I add, "Oh, one more thing Sarah, who else do you know that also owns a salon that if I mentioned your name would at least take a brochure from me?"

Almost always, one name pops out of their mouth.

"My friend Brenda owns Paradise Spa in Bedford, I used to work for her".

As part of my 'system', you gradually get 'invited' into larger businesses. You see, the name that pops out of her mouth is most often their former employer. We just enrolled a salon with 4 hairstylists, but Brenda owns that salon across town that has 24!

At first, you might think that this new little salon is actually Brenda's 'competition', and possibly a less-than-friendly competitor, but in reality it's usually just the opposite. Very often, 'Brenda' mentored the new salon owner, and they're probably still friends to this day.

If you just enrolled a 6-man plumbing outfit, and on the way out you say, "One more thing Joe, who else do you know that's a plumber in the Bedford area that if I mentioned your name, they'd at least take a brochure from me?" Joe's former employer literally 'apprenticed' him, and they are undoubtedly still cordial. In fact the 2 of them probably still go out to dinner together with their wives. But Joe's former employer, 'Steve's Plumbing' may very well have 26 plumbers and office staff to present to and enroll, not 6.

Without that referral, that business may very well have been harder to crack, because the bigger the business, the more likely they are to have a 'gate keeper', an HR department, etc. But with the power of a name (a referral) your chances go way up.

And remember, understanding the psychology of what we are and are not saying is crucial. I 'didn't' say, "Could you give me a list of people you know that I could bug and try to sell insurance to...and will probably be mad at you for giving me their names?" Alright, nobody does it that bad, but a lot of times that's what your client hears when you ask for a referral.

But when one particular name comes to mind (usually his/her former employer) the visual we created was us 'handing them' a brochure. What's the harm in that? Of course we are actually going to book 5 minutes with 'Joe' to 'go over' the brochure, but the visual is harmless.

Also note that I did not ask "Do you know anybody...?" but rather "Who do you know that...". One is a yes or no question, (which we don't want), while the other beckons a response.

So now we have a referral to go see...'Joe's Plumbing'. We look it up on Google and learn that it's located in the East-Side Industrial Park across town. We cross over to the east side, and see the 'Joe's Plumbing' sign, smack dab in the middle of the park.

Where's our very next stop? Joe the plumber right?

No!

We go to the first business in the park, American Roofing, and say, "Hey, how are you? I haven't had a chance to meet you yet. I'm Jonny and I work for a lot of your neighbors. I'm actually just a little early to see Joe at the plumber's, so I figured I'd meet a few more of the neighbors. After I meet with Joe, I am on the way to Boston today, but I think I'm back in town one more time, I think next Thursday. Say... If I stop by and catch you, can you give me 5 minutes with a brochure? You've seen the Aflac duck on TV right?"

"Of course."

"Great, what's your name?"

"David".

"David, good to meet you. Have a great day!"

Bam! You just used Joe's name (who you haven't even met yet) to land another appointment. It's what we always do, but this time you say it with just a little more conviction, because after all, we really 'are' there to see Joe.

Now don't be dishonest and say Joe's your customer already. He very well may be soon, but he's not yet, so don't say something that's not. If you ever are found out to be dishonest, that would be hard to recover from. We are merely dropping some insinuations.

However, the pressure's off American Roofing, because you're not really there to sell them anything. Why are we there? We are a little early to see Joe, and figured we'd meet a couple neighbors. How threatening is that?

Now you do the same thing with the next door, Sally's Diner, and then Tim's Speed Shop, and Tina's Doggie Daycare.

'Now' we go see Joe, and it sounds something like this…

"Hey, you must be Joe. I did some work for Andy in Manchester, and he asked me to stop by if I was ever in this area and show you what I did for him. Unfortunately, I'm on the way to Boston today, but small world, next Thursday I'm actually meeting with David at the roofing company. Say, when I get done with David next week, if I have time to stop by and happen to catch you, can you give me 5 minutes with a brochure to show you what I did for Andy? You've seen the Aflac duck on TV right?"

"Yes."

"Great, have a nice day."

You used Joe's name to book 5 appointments before you got to him, then you used the credibility of those 5 names, coupled with a referral…Joe doesn't stand a chance! That one 'warm call' just turned into 6. Now, after booking Joe's appointment, since you've got the mojo going on...meet 5 more neighbors on the other side, and you my friend have just done the "1-11".

That one referral just netted 11 appointments. I can't tell you how many times I've done exactly that.

But let's say we're just starting the day, and we're 'not' armed with a referral. Now where do we start?

You start at the very first business. Now the gatekeeper may tell you that the owner's 'unavailable' right now. That's fine. However, I add, "Okay, no problem. I was just hoping to introduce myself while I'm in town. I think I'm doing this route again in a few weeks. If I have time I'll try to stop back then. What's his name?"

The 'rejectionist' will almost always begrudgingly mutter the owner's first name, "Bill".

"Thanks, have a great day!"

But now at the next door, "Hey how are you? I haven't had a chance to meet you yet. I'm Jonny the Aflac guy. Bill next door is still in a meeting, so I figured I'd meet a couple neighbors while I'm waiting..."

I used Bill's name anyway!

Other times, the boss actually isn't there, but it's still going to help.

Perhaps 'Jim' is at the auction buying cars...

"Hi, how are you? I haven't had a chance to meet you yet. I'm waiting for Jim next door to get back from the auction, so I figured I'd meet a couple neighbors while I'm waiting. Once he gets back, I'm on the way to Boston, but I think I'm in town one more time next Tuesday. Say...If I stop by can you give me 5 minutes with a brochure? You've seen the duck on TV right?"

That's how the "1-11" happens even without a referral.

Remember, make a game of it.

One door at a time. One account at a time. And you're on the way to building a lasting dynasty and living the lifestyle of your dreams.

# Lunch and Learns

Okay, we've used a pretty simple approach, and added multiple stops to the milk (or bread) route.

But what if I could show you a way to actually skip the employer presentation, and go straight to an employee presentation and enrollment? Would you be interested?

Allow me to introduce you to the 'Lunch & Learn' strategy.

Now I've come to know many industries over the past 9 years, and have come to the realization that certain times of the day work for certain types of businesses. For example, the only time you want to enroll a daycare is at naptime. Almost any type of construction crew/landscaping/plumbing-HVAC etc. are dispersed across the state at all times of the day…except for first thing in the morning as they pick up their work orders and load up their trucks.

However, I was always frustrated with small medical and dental offices. I wanted to portray how busy 'I' was, but they actually always had a room full of patients sitting around the lobby waiting for their turn with the doctor. I knew their had to be a way to crack the code so to speak, and I really wanted to, since there are so many hundreds and hundreds of dentist and doctor offices everywhere.

But how?

I want to give credit where it's due, and in this case it goes to associate John Amero. He was willing to go through the trenches with me until we got it right. Through trial and error however, we learned to master the 'lunch & learn', and to date have probably written over 100 dental and medical practices. In fact, John Amero took off with it, and I doubt there's another agent that's closed for medical offices than he has.

Using my 'magic' opening line, with most industries, I can literally go to 10 doors and book 10 appointments. Once you master it, it works... (almost) every time. However, with what I am about to teach you, the numbers have been (almost to a science) right around 40%, but when it does work, it almost always leads right to an enrollment.

Now picture this. John Amero walks into a dentist office, with nothing but his date book in his hand, with his index finger already saving the month of May. He walks up to the reception desk, and says, "Hey, what do you have open for 'lunch & learns'" or better yet, "Who do I have to talk to, to buy you guys lunch?"

If the random person he chose to approach is not 'the one', he or she will immediately point to 'Sarah', the practice manager, (because she wants the 'free lunch').

"Hi Sarah, I'm John from Aflac. What do you have available for 'lunch & learns' 2nd week of May?"

Believe it or not, 'Sarah' usually looks at the calendar, and says, "Wednesday or Thursday".

Now just to play the game a little bit, whatever their 1st response is, I say, "Um, how about the week after that?", as I also open my date book. (Again, just to confirm how busy we are).

We agree on a day, I jot it down, and then close the datebook.

"Thanks Sarah", then grab a business card. "How many people are there so I know how much food to bring? And are you guys 12 to 1 or 1 to 2?"

You see, almost without exception, every doctor office (which includes pediatricians, podiatrists, surgeons, orthodontics, dentists, chiropractors, family PCPs…and even some veterinarians), actually lock their doors and shut off the phones every day for an hour.

Ironically, that would've been the one time you actually could see the doctor with the opening line, or the '5-minutes', but the door is locked.

'Practice managers' grew very accustomed to 'lunch & learns' thanks to pharmacy sales reps. Since Obamacare however, those free lunches are fewer and farther between. But who wouldn't want free lunch?

Now this is where 'assume & proceed' takes on a whole new meaning. The day of the appointment, order a few pizzas and a salad, pick up some drinks, cups, and napkins, and be sure to arrive at about '10-of'. Walk in carrying a bunch of food, and someone is sure to escort you to the break room.

I can't tell you how many times I've walked in and there is actually some kind of posted announcement or makeshift poster on the wall saying. "Aflac's bringing lunch Tuesday May 10th at 12:00". Sometimes you do need to give some preliminary instructions that your 'talk' is only about 10 minutes, "But please, start helping yourself to some lunch".

So many times I've educated the dentist, the hygienist, an assistant, and the secretary at the same time on 'how Aflac works'.

Especially if a couple employees don't get through with what they're doing until about 10-after, and keeping in mind that the next round of patients is due to start arriving at about 5-of, you need to go right into it. However, since I bought lunch, I usually do present 2 policies, typically accident and hospital, or accident and cancer. Of course I do also slip into my presentation that, "When you sit down with us real quick, you 'can' get quotes for dental, vision, life and disability…but in my opinion, these 2 are the most important".

Now the presentation itself is just the same as any other, but the close in front of the employees 'has to' end with very specific instructions.

Here it is…

"Okay, that's pretty much it. That's Aflac. If you were to get the same accident policy at your kitchen table, it might be close to $100/month for your family, but 'because' you are in the medical profession, you actually get the 3rd lowest rate in the country. Just $6.10 for the accident plan, and I think just over a dollar to add a spouse. When I sit with you for a minute, I can get your date of birth and tell you exactly the price of the other one, but most of the plans runs between 5 and 10 dollars/week…some even less. Now your coverage won't start until June 1st, so we have plenty of time, but I won't physically be back here again before then, so if you think you even 'might' want to get it, at least sit with me for a minute. I have to quote you a price in person, but we can do the rest over the phone." (Now I raise my own hand). "Does anyone need to go 1st because you have a patient coming in?"

I'm telling you, someone will either volunteer, "I'll go", or else say, "Suzy, why don't you go 1st, I think I just saw your 1:00 pull up outside".

Now you may be asking yourself about the AOD call. Of course. My last instruction is, "Okay I do need someone to do a quick 3-way call with myself and Aflac, for compliance, so they know we really are a dental office, not pretending to be just to get Aflac ½ price. Suzy, can that be you? I just need the tax-ID".

You do need to read the body language of the physician. Much more often than not, they see that the employees 'want it', and he or she is glad to let them 'get it'. At some point, just put your finger up and get the doctor's glance, and quietly ask (assuming), "Are you okay doing a payroll deduction for this? It's simple, and I can set it up with Suzy, and it doesn't cost you anything…in fact the practice actually saves some money in FICA savings?" There's usually no hesitation with that. If there is, say, "No problem, they can use debit cards" and drop it. (I highly recommend Piedmont Pays at this point if necessary, but we'll touch on this in a later chapter).

Sure, this entire scenario takes some 'kahunas' to roll out, but it's a rush! I lost count years ago just how many 'lunch and learns' turned into very profitable accounts for us.

It is a little bit of a gamble, and a tiny investment, but it's so worth it.

I can probably count on one hand the times these offices got 'free lunch' yet I didn't get an account, but so what. It usually works.

And please don't let the cost of the food prevent you from utilizing this approach. It doesn't have to cost a fortune. Many cities have a Little Caesar's, which is really inexpensive. You save a little by getting the drinks at a grocery store ahead of time, rather than from the restaurant. But even if you go 'all out' and spend $75, that 1st employee you enroll will net you $100, if not $200…and the rest of the practice is pure profit. Keep the receipt though, and at the end of the year you write it off as 'entertaining clients'.

I remember when I was a DSC, running with 2 to 4 new agents in the same quarter. Well that left very little time for my own cold-calling and appointments, so I'd do 1 or 2 of these 'lunch & learns' each month for myself, just to make sure I still had a couple thousand dollars coming in every month for cash flow, and at the same time being sure to add additional stops to my own 'milk route'.

You'll be amazed at how many times you'll be able to pull this off. And right before you leave, be sure to ask the dentist, "Thanks again Dr. Ray for allowing us to come in today" (which is actually kind of funny, because at least ½ the time he had no idea, because we simply booked it with the practice manager), "but what other dentist do you know that we could buy lunch for?"

Another stop on the milk-route.

A quick mention about not being afraid to invest in your business. As a rule, when you give, it comes back to you. (We'll also be revisiting this later in the 'Millionaire Mindset' chapter).

Even when arriving at 7:00am to present to a small crew of landscapers, I love to show up with a 'Box 'o Joe', and some munchkins or donuts. That $20 gesture certainly helps gather the guys (the old adage : "bring food-they will come"), and by the time everyone's chowed down a donut and had a coffee, I'm done talking…I raise my own hand and say, "Now does anyone need to go first because you have to get on the road?"

# More Tricks of the Trade

As I've FINE-TUNED MY system over the years, there are a few more evolutions I'd like to share with you.

For starters,

## PRESENTING YOURSELF AS A SPECIALIST

Suppose you owned a hair salon, and a gentleman walked in and said, "Hi, I'm Jonny from John Paul Mitchell…" Would the owner be at all surprised or put off by his arrival and introduction? Not at all. A person who sells shampoo and hair products is 'supposed' to be there.

Okay, now listen to this. "Hi, I'm Jonny, I haven't had a chance to meet you yet. I specialize in benefits for salons here in New Hampshire. Unfortunately, I'm on the way to Hampton today, but I'm doing this route one more time next Thursday. Say, if I stop by in the morning, could you give me a couple minutes with a brochure? You must always be looking for ways to attract the best hairstylists right?"

"Great. What's your name?"

"Sally. Good to meet you. Have a great day!"

Okay, for all you doves and owls out there let me let you off the hook a little bit. I really 'do' specialize in benefits for salons. I know what times are usually best to enroll them, and I'm fully aware that there's actually a good chance that they close altogether on either Monday or Wednesday. I am well aware of the 'dangers' of the profession. There's bleach that can splash, and there are very sharp clippers. There are also sore backs from reaching over a chair all day. I also know full well that in addition to accident policies being a given…hospital or sickness policies fill a need for maternity benefits, otherwise not available to hairstylists that usually are 1099. Cancer policies are next. I 'do' in fact have experience, having enrolled well over 50 salons in my career, and that in fact qualifies me as a 'specialist'. But the truth of the matter is that I became a specialist the moment I enrolled my 1st one. Becoming a specialist is actually a choice. I 'chose' to specialize in that particular industry.

It just so happens that I also chose to specialize in offering benefits to…

Daycares and preschools, landscapers, restaurants, volunteer fire departments, medical and dental offices, and real estate offices…just to name a few.

I highly recommend you become a specialist in several industries as well.

The magic is 'owning it' from the very 1st opening line.

## BACK DOORS

Again, giving credit where credit's due, one of the DSCs in my region, Tonya Manfrate, learned early on that the best way to get past the receptionist (rejectionist), is to avoid her altogether.

Whatever market you find yourself in, there are sure to be multiple industrial parks. What's nice about canvassing an industrial park is the sheer number of businesses within such a close proximity. Just a couple rows of buildings can often represent literally several dozen businesses. But almost everyone has a glass front door, and a gate-keeper just inside.

However, as Tonya discovered, most have garage/overhead doors around back. Going in this way, for one, avoids the receptionist altogether. And for two, most of the time the owner is under a hood, running a machine, or at a work bench himself. Remember, we are not approaching giant businesses (yet) where the owner is unreachable, and is probably on a yacht somewhere. These are small businesses where the owner is an average guy or gal, doing their best to make a living like you and me, but at the same time pursuing the American Dream by being self-employed.

As you enter the back bay, sometimes you can just tell which one's the owner. Other times it's not so obvious and you have to take a best guess, but at least you get to talk to a real person.

Many times if you say to an employee, "Hey, you must be the owner", even if it's painfully obvious that the person you are talking to could 'never' own a business, that little bit of flattery will likely get you some useful information... like, "Not me, Pat, the big guy with the moustache out front. You can't miss him".

After thanking the worker bee for the name of the queen, I head up the back hallway, toward the offices, coming 'from' the warehouse. The funny thing is many times I'll notice the back of the head of the lady positioned at the end of the hall, facing the front door. But I'm looking left and right, scoping out for a big desk and/or the 'big guy with the moustache'. As soon as I spot him, I immediately reach out my hand, and go right into the opening line, "Hi, I'm Jonny. I haven't had a chance to meet you yet…". Same as always, get your "Yes" (to the duck question), and go…back the way you came, out the rear warehouse door. Listen, very few sales reps take this 'bold' approach, so they are absolutely 'not' bombarded with salespeople. And besides, remember we just "haven't had a chance to meet you yet". Honestly, he may want to hire you as a sales rep!

But next week, when we come back, you actually 'do' go in through the front door, and greet the receptionist with a smile. "Good morning, can you tell Pat that Jonny's here?" Immediately break eye contact and sit down. It works!

Go try it, and you'll amaze yourself. Just remember to contain your enthusiasm when it does work. And 4 minutes later…you just booked an enrollment!

## USING 3rd PARTY ADMINISTRATORS

Lastly, I want to mention Piedmont Pays one more time. There are certainly other TPAs (3rd party administrators) out there, but in my opinion none nearly as user-friendly as Piedmont, and especially 'Aflac' user-friendly.

I believe the founder was in fact an Aflac RSC for a decade, if not more. After speaking multiple times with both Tim and Brian, let me assure you that they know their stuff, and they offer a real solution that works. (I'm not being paid to endorse them by the way). I learned that Tripp Amos recently invested significantly in the company. What better endorsement can you get than that? Their website is extremely Aflac-centered, and the operators that assist with the AOD calls actually ask you if you are utilizing Piedmont.

If you are unsure what I'm talking about, allow me to explain. There are instances where employees definitely want to purchase Aflac, but for one reason or another, HR, the owner, or some other decision maker at the company has a problem with taking payroll deductions. Other times it's not the company, but the industry itself (such as fast-food) where turnover is high. Some industries are seasonal, like landscapers and campgrounds. Being proactive here by utilizing Piedmont not only protects your no-pay (which could cost you a free trip to National Convention), but actually keeps your business on the books for a long time.

Now Aflac 'does' have a similar solution called EDB (employee-direct-bill). To the best of my knowledge, John Amero and I have written more EDB accounts than anyone else in the company. It used to work great, but HQ has added extra steps, delayed commission pay-outs, and the verification process has become rather clunky, to put it mildly. For non-technically adept account managers, the on-line registration 'constantly' has to be reset. And if an employee enrolls through EDB, paying the premium via credit card, and perhaps they reported their card lost or stolen, or the expiration date ages out…you only 'discover' what happened when you get a charge-back on your next monthly statement. Then, if the employee actually wants to reinstate coverage, they'll owe several months of back premium…often times an unrealistic amount for a fast-food worker to pay as a sum. And quite frankly, where EDB can 'only' draft once-a-month, $60/month is harder for a waitress to budget than '$14/week', for the same coverage. And to top it off, let's say you enrolled an employee on

May 5th, and they asked for a draft date of May 10th, then May 10th also becomes their effective date. But what if the account manager (HR) doesn't 'get around' to verifying that employee on-line, until the following Monday, which is actually May 12th...guess what happens? That employee's effective date just became 'June 10th', and it defaults to the following month. For one thing, you're not going to get paid until June 10th, and that policy stays in pended for weeks. And actually, your commission can be paid up to 10 'business days' after a successful draft! And what if that employee actually gets hurt on May 12th, and thinks he has coverage?! Guess what? That's not only a denied claim, but a ticked-off employee, and probably a very upset HR and/or business owner who now thinks Aflac's unethical! Oh yeah, what if you made an error entering the routing number or credit card info, and had just 1 number off, and the draft is unsuccessful? Will Aflac allow you to correct it?...No! You have to actually rewrite that employee again!

Did I mention there are issues with Aflac's EDB process?!

Actually, my pen just flowed on that last part, and I didn't actually realize that I had that much pent-up emotion from all my previous experiences, but did you feel my frustration there?

But the solution is 'NOT' walking away from that enrollment opportunity. The solution is Piedmont Pays.

With Piedmont, employees get a 'draft' on the same day they get paid. It can be set-up weekly, bi-weekly, or whatever their pay cycle happens to be. So their $10.42 'drafts' the same day their paycheck gets direct deposited, so it feels like a payroll deduction. And if it so happens that the funds aren't there for whatever reason (maybe they didn't get a paycheck on a vacation week), Piedmont does a 'soft' draft attempt…3 times. Then, if it's still unsuccessful, they reach out to that employee (and the agent) to find out the issue, and offer to do a make-up draft the following week, or even spread it out over the next couple of weeks!

Now 'that' can help keep the employee's coverage in place, and your business on the books.

Two of my daughters waitress. They are more loyal to themselves than to a particular restaurant, and in fact bounce between establishments…going wherever the work is. If one restaurant is currently offering more hours than another, that's where they'll work more shifts.

But what if the 1st restaurant, where she was working when she picked up that accident and vision policy, gets slow. If 'Outback' is really busy right now and offering more shifts… she moves. On traditional payroll, chances are those policies just lapsed. With Piedmont… it's business as usual, the coverage remains in place, and you keep getting paid.

Those seasonal landscapers can keep their Aflac when winter comes. They still have their coverage in place as they move into 'snow removal' season.

I would have to say that the #1 frustration I've had over the years in my Aflac career has been 'billing issues'. Listen, 'every' business has issues and obstacles. Every company has strengths and weaknesses.

Nobody will 'ever' supersede Aflac's ability to pay claims…ever!

But there can be billing issues.

Have you ever had an account pay their bill, only to receive a 'refund check', and every employee received a letter in the mail notifying them that their coverage had lapsed? I'll bet you have. Does that make for a happy customer? Not at all. At times like this, you have to do serious damage control...and 'hope' to save the account. Granted, the company 'underpaid' by $30, yet didn't indicate 'which' employee actually terminated. Now it 'is' the employer's fault...but then again, customer service Golden Rule #1, "The customer's always right". So how does that work out?

And to be fair to Aflac, 'all' carriers have billing issues.

But what if, on a case-by-case basis, you wrote accounts that 'never' got a bill?

I heard there's a DSC (I think in either Tennessee or the Carolinas) that actually writes 'every' case using Piedmont. That's an extreme stance, but hey, he never has billing issues!

I think with pre-tax savings and other advantages of payroll deductions, it usually makes sense to go that route. But certainly on a case-by-case basis, determine which businesses make the most sense to utilize what Piedmont does as a perfect solution.

We also utilize the Piedmont option to resurrect 'former' Aflac accounts. Look, sometimes the owner and HR like you, believe in the brand, love the duck, but a personal billing nightmare (at least in their own mind) was just unforgivable. "What if we could offer you the exact same coverage, but this time you never have to see an invoice?" It works.

Now one limitation is disability. You can't offer STD when utilizing a TPA, but you can offer everything else. I don't think that's a big deal at all though. I believe that even when an employee wants short-term disability, that they are 'really' saying that they want money if they ever get hurt or sick. Well most often, and accident, hospital, and cancer policy will do just that. In fact, in some of the industries we're talking about (like waitresses), STD only insures their 'check', which is nominal at best. 90% of their 'income' is actually from tips. If they actually receive a $2000 tax-free claim check from an Aflac hospital policy after having a baby, that sure feels like disability to them. Just make sure you clarify what it is and what it isn't, and it becomes a non-issue.

Now how does Piedmont get paid? Simply, by the employee. Piedmont Pays charges $6/month to do what they do. Whether that employee just buys an accident policy, or loads up on dental, vision, and hospital as well… it's still $6/month. That equates to $1.39/week. What we do is simply add that amount to the 1st policy (almost always accident) when we quote it. If the 'B' rated accident is $5.50/week, now it's "only $6.89/week…it's amazing". Not a big deal at all.

Piedmont now collects the funds, receives the invoice, reconciles with Aflac, and submits the payment for the premiums.

Please don't walk away from a terrific money-making opportunity just because the enrollment conditions or payroll situation is less than perfect…use Piedmont!

And their enrollment form couldn't be simpler. It's one page.

Fax or scan it to Piedmont, make everybody's effective date "June 1st", let Piedmont know what days payroll actually occurs, and 'you' get paid your advance the next day just like you would with any other payroll group.

And…another stop on the milk route.

# The Best Part-Time Job in America

To ANYONE IN SALES, what does 'ABC' stand for? "Always Be Closing". Well in the Aflac world, as true as that awareness needs to be, it also stands for something else…'Associate Bonus Club'. And we like bonuses!

Arguably the best part-time job in America is simply nominating somebody you believe has potential, and would possibly be a great candidate for this amazing Aflac opportunity.

Allow me to tell you Krista Prue's story. Associates Scott and Heather Huntley regularly frequented a customer in the Bangor, Maine area, a dental practice. Whether it is to assist with a claim or enroll a new hire, many of us get pretty familiar and friendly with our clients seeing them on a regular basis. I don't know if it was demonstrating how much fun life is for an Aflac agent, or rolling through pictures on their phones of recent trips to Cabo, Hawaii, Costa Rica, New Orleans etc. Whatever it was, one particular dental hygienist wanted to drink a little of whatever Heather and

Scott were drinking. She literally asked one day, "Do you think I could do that?", to which Heather and Scott replied, "Of course you could!"

Now normally, when an interviewee looks at the Aflac opportunity, and agrees to study for their insurance license, we encourage agents to pass their exam, and 'then' give their 2-week notice to their current employer.

Krista has had one job her entire life, being a dental hygienist in the Bangor, Maine area. Her 20-year career had gotten her to the point where she was in the $60,000+ range, certainly respectable, especially for northern Maine. And that also added a certain amount of security for this mother of two. But deep down Krista wanted something more, and Aflac proved to be that opportunity that she wasn't about to let pass by. Krista gave her notice that day!

I believe because she 'burned the bridge behind her' so-to-speak, she was 'all in', and she went on to write overt $500,000 in her 1st 12 months! That put over $150,000 in her pocket in 1st year commissions (not to mention $50,000 more in 2-to-12 trailer money, renewals, and stock!).

But this chapter is about nominating. The reason Krista's story came to mind, is I saw one of Heather's monthly ABC checks...and it was for $2,911!

If you nominate someone to the Aflac opportunity, you get a 5% override on their gross production, for an entire year. Think about it, Heather's ABC bonuses for nominating Krista tallied over $25,000!

Where else can you pick up a 'part-time' job that pays over $2000/month? Only in America. Only with Aflac!

Now Krista may in fact be a Superstar. She has continued her momentum, won multiple trips, and actually just returned from President's Club in Aruba!

Krista bought my 1st book "You Can Too" when she started, and closed 52 accounts in her 1st 12 months! If you asked her for the 'secret' (which I did in the pool last week in Miami) she'll say, "Book 10-Run 10!" Sound familiar?

Granted, Krista (ironically a self-proclaimed shy introvert, with a dreadful fear of public speaking), is still above average, and may not be your typical Aflac rookie, despite having zero sales experience whatsoever.

But let's just say you nominate 2 associates who pursue an Aflac career. Let's say one doesn't quite have the immediate success Krista had, but writes a mere $120,000 (which puts a little over $53,000 in their pocket 1st year). Let's say the second nominee wrote just $40,000. Well that's $160,000AP, but more importantly about $8000 for you! That's an average monthly ABC check of $600+/ month…enough to cover the payment of just about any car you want to drive!

Another ABC success story is Tim Wakeman (from my 1st book). Tim nominated Brock Coleman. Brock was a prison guard, who 'hated' his job, and especially his immediate supervisor. He had proudly served in the US military, and now found himself employed at the prison. Tim actually enrolled Brock for Aflac at the jail, and ended up nominating Brock after sharing the highlights of what the opportunity had to offer. And since…Brock has become the #1 account opener in the entire Market! He not only didn't wait to get licensed before giving his notice…he quit that day!

I believe with everything in me though, that like Krista, because Brock 'burned the ships', he was assured success.

In fact Brock qualified for FireBall (and the $3000 bonus that comes with it) 3 weeks ahead of schedule, which means he earned well over $9000 in his 1st 10 weeks'

He's sure to have an established 'milk route' faster than most.

But who else benefits from Brock's success? Tim! Just by offering Brock the opportunity to attain financial independence for his young family, Tim already netted well over $1500 in ABC bonuses from Brock's success, before Brock even completed his 1st quarter with Aflac.

That's amazing, and that 'HAS' to be the best part-time job in America!

# A.I.S. Factor

WE ARE SUCCESSFULLY AND repeatedly creating something out of nothing many times when we implement our sales skills and strategies to corral the employees. Countless times disinterested employees do a '180' once the lightbulb goes off, and they become your greatest ally in making sure all the other employees, "Gotta see the Aflac guy".

However, as we progress, we can start to implement a few key 'EDGE' strategies as we pivot from the employees' needs, to ways to assist that small business owner. Allow me to share a few ideas that cost you nothing, but guarantee every employee sits with you for at least 5 minutes. We call this the 'Butts-in-the-seats' or 'Asses-in-Seats' (pardon my slang)…AIS Factor.

We know that if we can just have a couple minutes with each employee, almost every employee will 'get it'.

## EMERGENCY CONTACT INFO

"By the way Ms. Employer, there are a few free services our agency provides to our clientele. When was the last time you updated the emergency contact info for your employees? Is that something you do regularly? What if one of your workers gets hurt on a job site or takes a fall in the warehouse, and they are being ambulanced to the hospital… do you have his wife's new cell phone number? Maybe not. No problem. Since we are sitting with the employees anyway, we can update that information for you. We don't do anything with the information, we simply gather the info and hand you the forms. We're glad to do it…"

Bam! Now you're not only offering insurance to the employees, but now you are providing a valuable service to the business owner. And what does it cost you? Nothing. But now you're assured an 'AIS Factor' of close to 100%.

## BENEFICIARY UPDATE

This one's powerful. Let's say that during our conversation with HR, as you reviewed what benefits they already have in place, you discover that they currently provide a $25,000 term policy for every employee. (Of course the fact is that it's almost never 'portable', so additional Aflac life may have significant value, but let's save that strategy for a later conversation).

"Mr. Employer, you mentioned that you actually already sponsor a term-life policy for each employee, and that's fantastic. However, when was the last time you rolled out a 'beneficiary update'?" (It's usually 'never' other than the original enrollment). "We learned the hard way unfortunately. We had a bank teller in NH, madly in love and engaged to be married, who naturally named her fiancé as her beneficiary. But later, apparently somebody cheated on somebody, and there was a pretty nasty break-up. Well years later, that lady was happily married to someone else, and had a new baby. Unfortunately she tragically died in a car accident. But because the break-up had been so bitter, the former fiancé, who was still listed as the beneficiary, didn't give the family a dime! Life changes. Employees may have had children since getting the life insurance policy. Or, perhaps their kids are now over 18, and it makes sense to make a change now. And we know that 50% of marriages end in divorce. No worries. Even though it's another carrier, we'll update that for you, and again, simply hand you the information. After we leave, if there are any changes, you and/or the employee will need to contact the carrier, but we'll get the information updated. "

And listen to how I pour this on afterwards…

"And Mr. Employer, I can't tell you how many times I've asked for a show of hands, 'Who told your beneficiary that there even was a policy?' Usually very few hands go up. And then I add, 'And who, when that policy came in the mail, put it in a fireproof metal box?' Usually one. Mr. Employer, this will also remind your employees of the value of what you are offering".

Bam…A__es in the seats!

## EMPLOYEE INFORMATION

"You know Ms. Employer, with the opioid crisis in America as bad as it is, you have employees that are driving your trucks. If they don't show up to work for days, you at least want to get your truck back. You may be unaware that they have recently been evicted, or moved, or even changed cell phone numbers…by updating this information we can at least help you get your truck back!"

I've never had an employer not appreciate that one.

Now some HRs are extremely proactive, and they have systems in place to regularly update employee info, emergency contacts, and beneficiary updates. But most do not. And even if they do, maybe this is something that you can offer to take a little off her plate. And what if this was an 'annual' service that you provided? That means you get to sit with every employee, at least once a year, and review not only the value-added services we are now providing, but also what coverage they currently have, offer claims assistance…and inform them of new policies that are available…a.k.a. upsell!

Below I've included a form that we created which actually incorporates all 3 of the strategies we just went over. It's a simple 1-pager, and you can print the company's name across the top…or better yet, paste the company's logo up top.

But these 3 strategies are actually very valuable services that you are providing for that company, while at the same time guaranteeing you an 'AIS Factor' of close to 100%.

## Employee Benefit Enrollment Information

| Employee Information |
|---|

Full Name: _____
          Last                                    First                          M.I.      Suffix

Preferred Phone: _____    Email Address: _____

Mailing Address: _____

Birth Date: _____ / _____ / _____

Spouse's Name: _____

Spouse
Coverage     Yes [  ]     No [  ]   Dependent Children
                                     Coverage:          Yes [  ]        No [  ]

| Life Insurance Beneficiary Information |
|---|

Beneficiary
Name: _____  Beneficiary Date of Birth: _____

Relationship: _____

City: _____        State: _____

| Emergency Contact Information |
|---|

Full Name: _____
          Last                                    First                          M.I.

Address: _____
         Street Address

         _____
         City                                              State        ZIP Code

Primary Phone: _____ Alternate Phone: _____

Relationship: _____

Employee Signature: _____

Date: _____ / _____ / _____

Now where these 3 literally cost you nothing, except for 2 minutes of your time with each employee, there are a couple other strategies that I've also implemented that have worked wonders.

## DISCLAIMER:

*Check with your state-specific DOI for clarification, but as long as no purchase is required, usually a $2 to $3 giveaway is more than acceptable.*

## RESTAURANT.COM

Let's face it, despite our best efforts, sometimes you still feel like the 'Leper in the Lunchroom', just hoping that someone stops by your Aflac booth or table wanting Aflac.

But to peak curiosity…people love free stuff!

One thing I've done is post a sign that says, "Free $25 Restaurant Gift Card just for getting a free quote".

It 'has' to be no purchase necessary, but what does 'getting a free quote' look like? …"Now let me just put your name and DOB into the computer and I'll get you a quote…" And give them the 3-minute version from chapter 6. This is another strategy that can work wonders.

Whether they purchase or not, thank them, and give them a restaurant card.

If you're unfamiliar with Restaurant.com cards, you can purchase them (depending on the quantity) for about $3/each. The employee then goes to 'Dine.com', enters a zip code and a list of participating restaurants pops up. They simply click on the restaurant of their choice, and they can print off a $25 restaurant coupon, and they bring it with them when they dine out. It may cost you $3, but it is perceived as a $25 value to the employee, which it is. As long as you've taken the time to master the '3-minute' presentation, you'll write a ton of business.

I remember when John Amero and I wrote a hospital, without the best conditions set. We set-up posters that read, "Free talking duck to the 1st 100 employees that get a free quote". That word spread like a virus throughout the hospital, and we wrote well over 100 employees, honestly to many who actually thought Aflac was car insurance, but were willing to get a quote just to own a talking duck! Those 3-inch talking ducks cost what, $3? But our ROI on that one was incredible. (And at the same time that investment raises money for the Aflac Cancer Center... truly a win-win!)

By the way, earlier that year, John Amero and I had gone through his goals (resolutions) for the year, in January. (If you know me at all by now, you can probably imagine that I take New Year's resolutions to a whole new level). Well together, we looked at the state web-site, and looked up the current records. At the time, the standing record by a level 01 associate for premium in a week stood at a little over $61,000. John decided that one of his goals that year was to break that record. Now it wasn't just a pipe dream...he wrote it down! I witnessed it, and that was that. At this point, John was still new, literally 6 to 8 months in the business. He had literally no idea how or where this 'goal' would come from, it's not like he already had something big lined up. Not at all. He had nothing at this point but desire. But that's the magic of it all, it works the other way. First you decide what you want, and 'then' you figure out how you'll get there. Well John went to work, and I believe opened 41 accounts that year, finishing in the top 10 nationwide. Now we wrote that goal down in January, but it was during the summer that John met another 'soccer-dad' in the bleachers during his daughter's practice. The other dad, Brian, eventually became a '3-accidents-and-out' sale for John a month or so later. Soon after, Brian referred John to Don, who was trying to make a name for himself as a producing broker at a local firm. Well Don worked with John and teed up an enrollment for a '5 Guys Burger and Fries' chain that had just come to NH. That went pretty well. So in November, of that year, in week 48, John and I used the 'Free Talking Duck strategy', and wrote that hospital in NH...and John wrote $62,400 in AP!! (Almost exactly what he had written as a goal 11 months earlier).

When you get real specific about what you want to accomplish, write it down, develop your skill set, and then implement simple proven strategies...look out world!

## DEPENDENT AUDITS

I remember speaking with Ian, STC of Ohio West, the first time that state had me out to teach my system. After my talk to the associates, I later chatted with Ian...swapping other successful strategies that each of us had had success with. He mentioned the incredible success they had recently had performing a 'dependent audit' for an entire school system. They saved the city of Toledo millions of dollars, and at the same time wrote incredible amounts of Aflac premium, thanks to this incredible AIS factor.

Here's the scenario. Imagine a school of literally hundreds of school teachers, janitors, and administrative staff. Of those hundreds of employees, what if even a few dozen were families whose child turned 26 during the previous year? Is that dependent child covered? If he is, he (or she) shouldn't be, because of the age cut-off. Not to mention, over the course of the year, that's many many thousands of dollars in extra premium payments, paying for ineligible children that have legally aged out. Furthermore, let's say hypothetically that 26-year-old kid has a major accident...to the tune of hundreds of thousands of dollars in claims? That drags down the 'claims experience' on the entire group the following year, all because of a claim that actually shouldn't have counted against their insurance in the first place, since that child should've aged out, and the next year, the entire school system sees a significant premium increase. Or...maybe that teacher who 'thinks' their oldest is covered, actually gets a denied claim at the hospital, and it leads to an inevitable bankruptcy because that teacher now has to foot the enormous hospital expenses out-of-pocket!

There's no good outcome there. That's where a dependent audit can be HUGE. You can perform a soft or a 'hard' audit (which requires birth certificates), but either way you can save that school system a fortune, and get every A__-in the Seat!

## CORE ENROLLMENT

Steve Karas, monster DSC is Massachusetts, also has experienced unprecedented success writing school systems, using a different AIS strategy. Steve uses electronic platforms to perform core enrollment. Simply put, teachers 'have' to see Steve and his team to get 'any' benefits, because the same platform also collects all the info for 'every' benefit the school system offers, from major medical, to 403(b), to dental…and Aflac. Sure, it's a little work to teach the team to explain and enroll multiple other carriers…but the AIS factor is incredible. They've written hundreds of thousands in AP!

Granted these last 2 strategies are much more complex and certainly need a good deal of training before you can implement them successfully. However, they are without a doubt opportunities that can give you quantum leaps of success. I'm not going to attempt to explain these 2 strategies in this book in detail, as it would not be doing it justice. Although, who would be more qualified to write such a case than an agent that has successfully closed hundreds of accounts, and been to the laptop thousands of times, progressively into larger and larger accounts using my "You Can Too" system? No one. Hone your skills, get to work, and visualize big things, and these opportunities are sure to come to you.

# Added Lines of Business

As the size businesses you call on progresses to a slightly larger clientele with even more employees, you'll want to present yourself more and more as an 'agency'.

Without question, the simplest 'You Can Too' approach, "You've seen the duck on TV right?" will net you dozens, and then hundreds of accounts, mostly in the small market. Our sweet spot of 3 to 25 employees is an endless hot market of countless industries, which includes 1099's, that desperately need what you have to offer. That 5-chair salon and that start-up landscaping company are often offering 'benefits' for the first time, thanks to you.

However, now I am going to introduce how additional partnerships can not only set the table, but start additional lines of income for you.

Thankfully, Aflac is not an 'exclusive' company, which would mean that if you are writing Aflac, you're not allowed to ever write with another carrier as well. This is a fine line here, and there is a lot of truth in the saying, 'Jack of all trades, master of none'. I believe Aflac should always remain your absolute primary focus and objective, but I also believe that certain other offerings pair up perfectly with what we are doing. (Like a nice red wine with a filet mignon).

NOTE : The average multi-millionaire has 8 lines of generated income. In a future chapter, I'm really going to speak to that mindset…covering things from storage units to rental properties as part of your 'portfolio'. But for now I'm going to mention 3 specific 'other carriers' that can contribute not only to your cash flow, but a more complete 'package' that you can offer to your clients.

A quick mention of Everwell and subsequent VAS (value added services)…Aflac is already trending this way as well. Several of these VAS are already built into Everwell, our most recent enrollment platform.

Complimenting the last chapter, simply offering EZ Shield, at no cost to the employer, can be a fantastic AIS Factor. If you position it correctly, you can use that to gain incredible access to the employees.

Some of Aflac's VAS are state specific, and others are only available, or at least more impactful, when you pivot to Aflac's 'Group' products. Simply go to 'benefitbuilder@aflac.com' and play with it to learn how programs like the 'medical bill saver' and the 'college assistance program' can be incredible AIS positionings, with help from your broker channel.

One of Aflac's primary value-added-services is Me-MD. Using this as your AIS can be awesome. There may not be any additional income generated, but it's the equivalent effect of using a $3.00 Restaurant.com card or giving away a duck, yet it actually cost you nothing.

However, allow me to introduce you to Ally Health. They have a program that actually brings employees to the same Me-MD portal, but can actually be 'sold', and can give the employees better access, at zero cost to the employee.

In case you're new to the idea of 'tele-medicine', let me back up for a moment and explain the concept.

Now this is definitely something I wish I had had access to back when I was a single dad raising 5 kids. I remember when my youngest daughter Cady would get ear infections. After the first time, I knew exactly what to look for. Once you see the temperature rise, the runny nose, swollen eyes, and red ears, it's pretty apparent that it's another ear infection. What I needed was Amoxicillin. That meant I needed to see a doctor. I could try and rush home and get to a walk-in clinic before they closed, but if I didn't make it in time, it's a visit to the ER, which cost even more money. My other option was a miserable long night, both for my daughter and myself because I was up with her, and then I'm missing work the next morning, bringing her to the pediatrician, still paying a co-pay.

If I had had Ally Health then (like I do now), I could've simply called Ally Health, spoken to a doctor over the phone (or Skype, Face-time, text etc.), describe the symptoms, and had a prescription for Amoxicillin called in to the nearest CVS or Walgreen's…all in about 10 minutes, without having to ever leave the house. My kid would have anti-biotics in her within the hour, and most likely already be much better by the morning…rather than just starting the medicine after hours in the pediatrician's office (full of other sick kids), the next day. Wow I wish I had had that!

Sometimes I joke with employers that, "These doctors 'almost' passed medical school. Just Kidding. These are board certified doctors that have their own practices, but rotate days to be available to answer Ally Health calls".

I remember writing a grocery store here in New Hampshire, and the reason they implemented Ally Health was the following scenario. Picture this…

A guy in the produce department is working as many hours as he possibly can, living paycheck to paycheck. He gets conjunctivitis, which is extremely contagious. However, once you start taking an anti-biotic, you are soon no longer contagious. But this guy (in his mind) couldn't miss a minute of work. Before long, picture an entire produce department with goopy, pink eyes. Gross! Had he had Ally Health, he could've called in while on a quick break, described the symptoms over the phone, and had a prescription called in within minutes. He could've run out at lunch, gone through the drive-thru pharmacy, started taking the medication, and possibly no longer be contagious by the end of his shift!

They put in Ally Health!

One last story (because stories sell), one of my agents, Renee, had a kid in college whose wisdom tooth was all infected, and was in agony. Mom had her child take a picture, send it to the Ally Health doctor, and dial in. Sure enough, a prescription was called in right at the campus pharmacy. Now it still required a trip to the dentist the following Monday, but the dentist was amazed, "How in the world did you already get an anti-biotic called in? Usually I would prescribe that today, and have you come back in a couple days…but I can actually pull that tooth today!"

Amazing.

Now, not that it's a deal breaker, but the biggest difference between Aflac's 'free' value-added-service, offering Me-MD versus directly selling Ally Health yourself is that Me-MD has a $25 co-pay per call. Ally Health never charges one. In fact it is 24/7 unlimited usage for everyone in your household (from grandchildren to grandparents living with you), still never a co-pay.

Now here in New Hampshire, the two major health insurance carriers, Harvard Pilgrim and Anthem, have both recently implemented some form of 'tele-medicine' into most of their plans. However, they usually experience a utilization rate of less than 4%. One major reason is the lack of education around it. If you just give an employee a tele-medicine card, without explaining exactly how to use it, it will be in their wallet, but the next time their kid wakes up screaming with a fever in the middle of the night… they're headed straight for the emergency room. Also, there's usually about a $45 co-pay. So employees most often think to themselves, "Why should I spend a $45 co-pay when chances are they're just going to say I need to be seen anyway, and pay 'another' co-pay?…forget it!"

With Ally Health we often see 20, 30, 35, even 40% utilization! The biggest difference…no co-pay!

Now 'after' the initial enrollment meeting, where you tell stories to the employees and teach them how and why to use their Ally Health cards, Ally Health continues a relentless 'drip campaign' reminding employees that they can save by using their Ally Health card. "No missed work. No co-pays." There are at least monthly e-mails that go out to each and every employee, as well as random ticklers, and even an occasional phone call. That makes a huge difference!

Also, when the employee gets to the pharmacy, they've been taught to ask the pharmacist to run their prescription both ways…once with their major medical insurance card, and second with their 'Ally Health prescription discount card'. Your regular insurance very well may have a 'tier-2' co-pay of $20, yet with Ally Health there are literally hundreds of medications that are under $5! The employee saves again. Now if your Ally Health discounted price is $12, and your insurance has a $10 co-pay, well that's 3rd grade math. Use the insurance. But more often than not, it will actually be less with Ally. A couple that works for me has Tri-Care military insurance, and they save over 50% on name brand medications with the program. Just last week, my wife's prescription was about to be $54 (with my Anthem insurance), but it literally dropped in half ($27) with my Ally Health card.

I will say that the first time I asked my local pharmacist to run my prescription both ways, she acted a little 'put out', and bothered at the extra work. However, her expression changed and I remember her eyebrows going way up when she realized that in fact I was saving quite a bit of money by using the discount card rather than my traditional insurance. She no longer rolls her eyes when I ask her.

Interestingly enough, once when I was educating the employees of a large plumbing outfit in Vermont, on everything from the accident policy to tele-medicine, one of the employees volunteered that he had just seen an episode of either "20/20" or "60-Minutes". The special was about the apparent 'gag order' on pharmacists in this country. It turns out that if you present your insurance card at the time you drop off a prescription, when you pick-up the script, the pharmacist may simply say "$60 please". However, had you presented the same script as a 'cash customer', there's a very good chance that that medication might have only cost you $35, because that constitutes the 'cash price'. At this particular enrollment, other employees also confirmed having seen the same program, and I guess that the standing 'gag order' (thanks to Big Pharma) states that the pharmacist can't 'volunteer' that there may be a lower cash price, but "if" you ask, then they are required to let you know. I certainly wasn't aware of that. So today, I actually ask the pharmacist to run my scripts '3' ways…with insurance, with Ally Health, and then the cash price. Yes, it will get you more eye rolls, but they'll do it if you make them. It pays to be an informed consumer!

So the pharmacy prescription discount card is another factor that differentiates Ally Health from the Me-MD given as a VAS via Everwell. There is no co-pay 'and' you save on prescriptions.

The third and final purpose of Ally Health is their 'medical negotiation' service. If an employee has an outstanding balance of hundreds or even thousands of dollars from a previous surgery or hospital stay, Ally Health will now also get on the phone with that hospital, and actually negotiate down the employee's balance significantly. Possibly even in half! Even if I knew all the medical codes found on an EOB, and knew just who to talk to, that takes a lot of time away from working because when are medical billing offices open? During the work day. So employees, even if they were trying to negotiate their own bills, would out of necessity be doing so during the work day. Another way we save time and money to both the employee and the employer.

Now there are times that the Ally Health doctor will have to say, "You know what, that could be a couple of things. I think you better go get looked at", but nothing ventured-nothing gained. And of course a tele-medicine call can't do much if you have a bone sticking out or need stitches, but think about how many times you 'could' use it.

1.  Conjunctivitis

2.  Urinary Tract Infections

3.  Poison Ivy

4. Ear Infections

5. Fevers

6. Colds

7. Flu-like symptoms

8. Aches

9. Acne

10. Rashes…just to name a few.

The first time you dial in, expect to spend about 5 extra minutes, answering the same questions you'd see on a clipboard at a new doctor's office…family history, allergies, etc. They are totally HIPAA compliant, but do share your information with one person, your PCP, to make sure they aren't writing a prescription that might counteract with a script your primary care has you on. After the first call, that information is saved in the system, so future calls take even less time.

I believe that Ally Health can be the magic silver bullet in both large and small cases. In a large group, say with 100 employees on the company's health insurance, I give the following scenario, "Mr. Employer, let's say that just half of your employees use Ally Health just twice in a 12-month period. From swimmer's ear, to a UTI, to a kid waking up with a fever in the middle of the night. But let's say they were able to get the medicine they needed without having to see a doctor. Not only did they not have to pay a co-pay or have to miss work, but think about what that could do to your claims experience. That's 100 claims that never hit your insurance! For employers over 50 lives, your 'experience rating' (the total number of claims during a calendar year) directly correlates to how much of a premium increase you see the following year. That's 100 less claims. Now let's say that just twice a year, ½ of your employees get a $2 generic price for a prescription by using Ally Health rather than use their insurance card. Well that's another 100 'non-claims'. Together, with 200 less claims, you might even see a premium 'decrease' next year!

In this scenario, you'll often get 'employer-paid' Ally Health, which is only $8/month per employee. That's a worthwhile investment that could literally result in saving thousands in premium dollars.

Your commission on that case of 100 lives is about $1/employee, or $100/month, for the life of the case. That's year after year. But much more importantly is the guaranteed AIS factor! You get to see 'every' employee, to explain both Ally Health, and Aflac!

Now, let's move back to a much smaller account. To test the results of these programs, I went into the front lines with my agents and got a first hand look at how effective they can be. I remember enrolling a gun shop with a new agent here in New Hampshire. I was really hoping to get an 'employer-paid' allowance for Aflac, but when it was all said and done, he just couldn't swing it yet, having just purchased the business less than a year prior. I quickly pivoted to Ally Health. Seeing the value of 'offering benefits' intrigued him, and he agreed to sponsor the Ally Health.

When we met with each employee, we said, "Hey, how are you? You must be Pete." (We had gotten a list of names of the 12 employees and walked around with a clipboard). "Listen, Scott is offering benefits to you guys now. He's actually paying for an Ally Health program for every employee, and making dental, vision, life, and disability and other programs available at like ½ price through Aflac!"

Most of them said, "No way! That's awesome!"

I 'pitched' the Ally Health by telling my daughter's ear infection story, and my agent with the kid in college/tooth story, then proceeded with, "What's the address you want your Ally Health card sent to?"

Then, "He's also making Aflac available to you at a huge discounted rate. Have you ever had Aflac before?" Then our 5-minute accident pitch, and a hint of other programs available.

'Every' employee at the gun shop at least picked up an accident policy, and I believe we wrote a cancer policy and a couple dentals as well.

At the end, I'd add, "Hey make sure you thank Scott for bringing us in okay?"

"Oh, I definitely will".

I never told them that Ally Health was only $8/month.

The following scenario is what I used to seal the deal with Scott to get him to sponsor the Ally Health in the first place. I asked him to envision the following hypothetical conversation with an employee...

"Hey Pete, I've got to say I'm extremely impressed with your performance here at work. You're the first one in, and often stay late if necessary without ever complaining. You help train new employees, and you're great with the customers. Listen, I want to do something for you. I'm going to give you a 5-cent/hour raise."

That would 'not' make an employee very happy now would it?!

But now listen to this conversation. "Hey Pete, I've got to say I'm extremely impressed with your performance here at work. You're the first one in, and often stay late if necessary without ever complaining. You help train new employees, and you're great with the customers. Listen, I want to do something for you. Unfortunately, I can't do a lot being my first year in business, but I really wanted to do something for you, so I have an insurance guy coming in. I've actually purchased an Ally Health program for you, and he also has all kinds of stuff like dental, vision, life, and disability that you can get at a reduced rate. Thanks for everything you do, really!"

Ally Health is actually the equivalent of only a 4.6 cent/hour raise, but which of the previous two conversations would be better received?

The gun shop was a home run!

Ally Health can also be employee-paid, and even payroll deducted. Like Aflac, you need 3 or more employees to participate, and it's only $2.95/week if EE-paid. We've used this strategy as well, and still had 100% participation, and my agents are still generating an additional line of revenue with Ally Health.

Also, Ally Health, as a company, is great to work with. Very easy to enroll, and they have instructional webinars on 'how to enroll a case' several times every month.

More than anything, it's a fantastic AIS Factor.

Also, in large cases, the price goes down significantly. A large chain of religious schools with hundreds of teachers got a rate of under $2/month per teacher.

One last way to incorporate Ally Health is in getting the initial appointment with that decision maker. My good friend, RSC Joe Calarco from New York, has had me out a couple times to teach my "You Can Too" system to his team. His son Nicholas, who is now a DSC, has incorporated Ally into his initial pitch. His line goes something like, "Hi, how are you? I'm Nick and I do benefits for a lot of your neighbors, representing companies like Aflac and Ally Health. Who does your telemedicine now?"

"Our tele-what?"

"I'll be in the area next week and in a few minutes I can show you how our programs work." One look on RPM, and you'll see he's crushing his new account metric.

This one simple tool can revolutionize your business.

## MEC PLANS

Being conversant in 'Affordable Care Act' language (or at least enough to sound like an expert) is extremely valuable.

One tenant of the ACA is the 'preventative care' clause. No matter where you buy your health insurance, regardless of which carrier, what level, or premium amount, preventative services have to be covered 100%. That's not just your annual physical, but your pap smear, mammogram, flu shot, kid's immunizations, blood work etc.

Another important tenant to keep in mind is the 'no pre-existing condition' clause. That simply means that even terminally-ill patients can purchase health insurance, with no underwriting, and cannot be denied coverage.

Now there are certainly some ludicrous parts to the ACA, like the only health question being, "Do you smoke cigarettes more than 3 days/week?" You can smoke a carton on Friday and Saturday night while you're drinking, and that would still qualify you as a non-smoker. You could also smoke 'funny stuff' 7 nights/week, and you're still a non-smoker! And even a declared cigarette smoker pays only a slightly higher premium.

However, there is a viable option, especially for smaller employers, which can be the saving grace in the marketplace.

MEC Plans: 'Minimal Essential Coverage'

In one sense you could say that a MEC plan is just terrible insurance. But actually, for around $74/month, it's actually pretty good insurance. Let me explain. What it 'does' do, is cover all of your preventative procedures (physicals, mammograms etc.), plus 1 other non-routine visit with your PCP/year. Then, most importantly, it's a national 'PHCS' PPO network. That means you get negotiated rates should you ever need an MRI, surgery, or hospital stay. So hopefully, you'll only have to pay $800 for that MRI, not $1800. And PHCS, (to the best of my knowledge), is accepted at every major hospital in the United States.

Now the one big hole in the MEC plan is that it does not have the 'out-of-pocket-maximum' to protect you. So there is an exposure to potential medical expenses should you have an accident, or need specialized long-term treatment for something. But at least if you do receive a dreaded diagnosis, thanks to you receiving your regular preventative procedures, since they 'are' covered, hopefully you catch that diagnosis early. Then if you do find out that you are going to be needing expensive medical treatments… "Quick, go buy regular health insurance!" Thanks again to the 'no pre-existing' clause, you can't be denied. Granted you may have to wait until the next open-enrollment, but this is still a very viable option.

Imagine…you notice your garage is burning, so as quickly as possible, you run out and buy really good home-owner's insurance! Or right 'after' a car accident, you call Allstate or Geico and say, "I need to lower my deductible for the month, because I just had an accident". Now of course in the P & C (property and casualty) insurance world, you could never do that. But with health insurance, you actually can!

(Now as I write this, I actually have mixed feelings on the entire subject, because at this point, health insurance isn't really insurance at all when you can buy it after-the-fact like this. And a quick shout-out to the Aflac PAC who really saved the day while all this was transpiring. Getting deeply involved with Congress, on both sides of the aisle, they made sure that for example, our cancer insurance couldn't be mandated to be 'guaranteed-issue'. Could you imagine what that would've done to both your sales and commissions? Simply put, people would just wait until 'after' they ever got cancer to buy our cancer insurance. So again, I have mixed feelings around this entire chapter, but we are merely capitalizing on a marketplace that is in desperate need of our help.)

As far as 'which' MEC plan to offer, there very well may be other good companies out there, but personally we have found APEX to be great. They actually offer 4 tiers of coverage, and the higher levels actually look and feel more like traditional health insurance, having for example a $50 co-pay for a walk-in clinic. Yet even their most expensive tier, even with family coverage, is still in the vicinity of $400/month. That's a whole lot less than a traditional family insurance where I've seen, even in a group, climb to close to $3000/month.

APEX has been great, and is easy to write, and their back-office help is extremely user-friendly. If you do choose another company, just make sure that it is truly a PPO, not just a TPA, so that you actually get the negotiated rates for medical care. APEX also offers 'rate locks' for 3 to 5 years! And finally, it 'can' be payroll deducted, and even taken 'pre-tax'.

Paired with an Aflac accident and hospital policy, that previously uninsured employee is way better off than before. Just be certain to explain what it is, and what it is not. Also, even though MEC plans 'do' satisfy the national mandate (which Trump is abolishing anyway come 2019), you still need to make sure it satisfies the mandate in your particular state. For example, in Massachusetts, unless an employee enrolls in Mass Health, the state's mandate is not met, even though a $22/month fine at the end of the year is 'way' less than potentially $2000 IRS fine at the national level. But remember, with no insurance, they were paying that fine anyway. At least now they have some level of insurance.

## OIL CHANGES

I often include my 'oil changes' discussion when addressing a group of employees about the MEC plans. Let me tell you about my dearest daughter Sophie. (You might remember her from my first book, where I mentioned her sprained ankle claim.) Well since, Sophie has blossomed into a beautiful young adult. However, in her teen years, as a relatively new driver and car owner, believe it or not she seized THREE engines, in one year, all because she never checked/changed her oil! (I'm totally serious!) Despite her mother and I literally nagging her to simply get her oil changes, she ignored it, until her car stopped working. I literally got the call, "Can you help me? I think I ran out of gas again." (which he also did more than once). Each time I arrived, and mentioned that the smell, the smoke, and the bright engine light have nothing to do with gas…,"You ran out of oil again!" I wish I was kidding. In the last couple years, I think she's finally learned, but before we pick on Sophie too much, how many people treat their health like that? If you wait until your 'car is smoking' so to speak, it's often too late. "Please get your oil changes" I echo, as I remind them that their MEC will pay for it 100%. "Better to find out you have cancer at stage 1 than stage 4!"

Now you may not get rich writing a MEC Plan, but it still contributes to your monthly residual income. You'll make approximately $10/month per employee enrolled. So, a group of ten enrolled, and that's another $100/month residual income. But more importantly...AIS! Of course you're pairing it with Aflac policies, so it should be a homerun.

## WHOLE LIFE INSURANCE

Do you have any idea what the mortality percentage is in the town you live in? You're not going to believe this...but it's 100%! LOL.

According to Aflac's Worksite Reports, close to 3 out of 5 employees would buy life insurance if their employer offered it through work.

There's an obvious need for it, and at the same time a great demand for it.

I've written hundreds of life policies during my tenure with Aflac. However, I've also gotten contracted with other carriers such as Kemper, Transamerica, and Boston Mutual.

Now Aflac is the 'best' at what they do best, from accident insurance to their cancer policy, to paying claims in just 1 day. Nobody else even comes close. However, if you think that a large manufacturer with 300 employees would ever replace their 'Delta Dental' traditional dental insurance for Aflac's supplemental dental, you're being naïve. Certainly it's great that our dental has no networks, and especially no participation requirements, and you can even layer our 'Basic' dental on top of a traditional plan to fill in the gaps of traditional coverage...but it is what it is, a supplemental program. (Our dental does work great. I used the Standard dental plan for my family for 8 years). But living in reality, there are times where other companies who 'specialize' in life insurance (just like Delta specializes in dental), may be a better fit. For example, my agency has an underwriting offer that gives even small employers (of 5 lives or more) guaranteed-issue life insurance. It's a whole-life product, and in most states includes long-term care as well! It's super easy to enroll (we use a 2-page paper app with all the health questions crossed off, thanks to GI), but more than anything else guaranteed-issue means AIS...you 'have' to see everybody. You'll write at least twice as much Aflac because you set the table with such an incredible life product!

Here's where you need to evolve into, and present yourself as, an 'agency'. My very good friend Joe Calarco helped me and my team embrace this entire concept. We've learned to cement ourselves as industry experts that have 'solutions'.

Rather than present yourself just as an Aflac guy or gal, you position yourself as an agency. I had my assistant (and I recommend you do the same) create a binder for me, and plastered across the front cover are the emblems of 'several' carriers on it, almost like a collage...including APEX, Ally Health, Transamerica, the Everwell Logo, Piedmont Pays, EZ Shield...and of course Aflac.

Now, by being that 'expert', representing multiple companies, offering multiple solutions, that business owner trusts and respects you more, and it's the ultimate AIS scenario.

Now there are still plenty of times where a single employee at a company just wants a $30,000 20-year term insurance policy for a couple of bucks/week. Aflac's the perfect fit in that scenario. However, learn to present and position yourself as the expert, and as an 'agency', and you will grow your business to a whole new level.

Going back to our simple "You Can Too" approach, where we did our magic opening line, a 4-minute ER days later, and soon after enrolled all six employees an accident policy, and upsold 2 dentals and a hospital at the laptop, and put over $900 in your pocket thanks to your Aflac advances. But then that 6-man plumbing outfit refers you to 'his' former employer, which turns out to be a 36-man operation, with an office staff, a small sales force, and several crews…well here's where we morph into the 'agency' mode. The referral is much more apt to listen to your solutions, especially if the referring business calls and tees it up for us. Don't miss this golden opportunity to incorporate 'agency' strategies to get every butt in the seats!

Aflac is absolutely going to continue to be your primary objective. And, especially in terms of long-term income goals, I haven't seen another comp plan out there that gets you vested so quickly, and pays level-renewals for life! However, there is actually a significant amount of money to be made writing these whole-life cases with other carriers. The first year commissions are astonishing, and can literally become even a secondary 6-figure income for you, but keep in mind that the renewals will be nothing like you see with Aflac. So don't allow yourself to get distracted just by earning quick commissions with other life carriers. That would be living very short-sighted. Instead never forget that your focus 'must' always be to continue to use these other strategies…as a table setter for Aflac. That's where your long-term walkaway residual income is going to be the largest, by far, for years to come.

## DEFINED CONTRIBUTION STRATEGY

Okay, let's picture yourself as a small garage owner, maybe you have 12 employees. You've never offered health insurance, and honestly, you've never had to.

But today, your best employee (your master mechanic) comes into your office and says, "Hey boss, I just had to pay a $2800 fine on my income taxes because I don't have health insurance. What are you going to do about it?", or maybe just, "Hey boss, my wife's constantly on me about getting health insurance 'cuz we're trying to have a baby. Can you help me out?"

Again, you've never had to offer benefits before, and quite honestly, it's not in the budget. In fact, after 6 years in business, you're 'finally' able to give yourself a regular paycheck. Now your employee wants you to buy health insurance…there's no way!

As much as you hate it, your hands are tied, and though you hate to see your best employee go, you're just going to have to replace him.

However, when you start interviewing qualified mechanics, one of the first questions they ask is, "Do you offer health insurance? Because my wife told me to make sure I asked".

All of a sudden, replacing that quality mechanic who left isn't so easy. What are you going to do? Perhaps there's no choice, and you're going to have to offer health insurance after all!

So what's the first step to even explore such a notion? You call in a 'broker' to give you prices on health insurance. "Maybe it's not that expensive" you think to yourself.

But that broker doesn't exactly tell you what you want to hear. Even with a medium to high deductible, the family plan runs close to $2000/month. "You're out of your fricking mind!" you tell your broker, who, no pun intended, seems to want to make you exactly that…'broke-er'. Even if you were to split that premium with your employees 75/25, which means you are paying $1500 per employee, and the employee pays the other $500, neither of you can really afford it. Yet, if you did go that route, and someone asked that employee, "How much does your health insurance cost?", they'd still say something like, "You wouldn't believe it if I told you. It's like 120 bucks/week out of my paycheck. It's probably illegal. It's ridiculous." Yet, they actually have no idea that you as the employer are actually paying the other $1500/month, (X's how many employees?). They just think that their $500 is a lot!

If you think the scenario I just laid out is fantasy, then you need to wake up, and realize what the need is, and most importantly, how to capitalize on it!

Now picture that employer (who just last week fell off his chair after getting prices from that traditional broker). You 'discover' his dilemma, and say, "Wow, I totally understand what you're saying Mr. Employer. We're hearing that more and more. However. 'is' there a number, that if benefits only costed 'X' amount, you'd actually be able to consider offering benefits to your employees?"

The number I have heard most often is, "Yeah, I was hoping for around $300/month".

"Mr. Employer, if I could show you a comprehensive benefit package that included health insurance, prescription discounts, unlimited access to doctors without a co-pay, a retirement savings plan, life insurance, dental, vision, disability…all for around $250/month, would you be interested?"

What do you think they say?!

It looks something like this:

# DEFINED CONTRIBUTION BENEFIT PACKAGE

## Through Creative Benefits

$74

+ $8

+$38

+$80

_____

$200

Menu of: Dental, Vision, Life, Disability, etc.

Okay, $74/month purchases an APEX MEC plan for that employee. Now all their preventative care is paid for 100%. They get an additional visit with their PCP, and they are part of the PHCS network, and will receive huge discounts on any other necessary medical expenses.

For $8/month, they now have Ally Health, which means unlimited access to doctors without a co-pay, to call in prescriptions. It also gives them access to hundreds of prescription medications for under $5. And… the medical negotiation service.

With $38/month, we're going to purchase as much Transamerica guaranteed-issue whole-life insurance as we can, based on their age and smoking status. That's probably enough for around $25,000 in life insurance. They will build cash value for retirement, and in most states also receive benefits for long-term care, should they ever become disabled.

Then…an $80/month allowance for Aflac! That's almost $20/week with not only AIS, but an allowance so that each employee gets to 'go shopping' with Aflac. Now I position with employers, "They can decide to purchase dental, vision, disability, maternity…whatever". Because that's what the marketplace 'thinks' they need or want, even though we are much more apt to steer the employees to use that allowance to pick up an accident and hospital policy to offset any unforeseeable medical expenses, particularly with a MEC plan.

And get this…it's a 5-year rate lock! We know Aflac premiums never change. Whole-life premiums are just that…for life. Ally Health is constant, and even APEX comes with a 5-year rate lock (I think they can only raise premiums 3% annually, compared to traditional insurance rates which can literally double, like mine did).

You can 'save' that business owner! And the employees absolutely love it. We've never seen employees so enthusiastic and appreciative of their employers before. It's amazing!

You are now armed with a strategy that can position you in such a way that you can absolutely dominate your local market, and make a fortune. Let's take a look at what kind of revenue we can generate utilizing this amazing strategy.

Let's envision enrolling a 12-man garage, like we proposed.

That's approximately $10/month per employee on the MEC plan. That alone is a $120/month instant residual income.

Ally Health, as inexpensive as it is, also pays around $1/month per employee. So there's another $12/month.

Now when it comes to the whole-life insurance, your commissions are typically front-loaded. That means that you're going to make a larger than normal commission up front, and less of a renewal, but it's quite a significant amount of cash flow. Now if 12 employees spend $38/month, that's $456 each annually...totaling $4,572 in annualized premium. Carriers may vary, but you'll receive at least 50% in 1st year commissions. Paid monthly, that's another stream of $228/month.

And finally, what kind of damage can you do when employees have a $20/week allowance for Aflac?!

If no employee went a penny over their allowance amount, that's still $80/month, or $960AP. X's 12 employees that's $11,520 in Aflac AP, all employer paid!'

The average commission being 35%, that's over $4000 net commissions. You'll receive a $2540 advance (within 2 days), and then another $135/month for the remainder of the year.

So let's see, you become a hero to that small business owner. Every one of the employees is thrilled. You receive an advanced commission of over $2500 within days, and you also created an additional instant monthly residual income of $495/month!

What if you landed just one of these cases each month. Nothing huge, simple 12-life cases. Using the same numbers, that's over $30,000 in advances, and $6000 in monthly residuals! That alone is a 6-figure income!

Now imagine this as a stop on your 'Milk Route', where every new hire is a 4-carrier, commission yielding, guaranteed sale!

Ready for this? What if you used '$250' instead of $200? I have a 2nd option that does just that, which bumps the whole-life allowance up to $48/month, and the monthly Aflac allowance to $120!

# DEFINED CONTRIBUTION BENEFIT PACKAGE

## Through Creative Benefits

$74

Apex Management Group

+ $8

 **Ally**Health
*"We're on your side"*

+ $48

 **TRANSAMERICA**

+ $120

**Menu of : Dental, Vison, Life, Disability Etc.**

_____

$250

By providing both options to the employer, you are actually asking a "Yes/Yes" question. Whichever they choose, you win, and you win BIG!

You'll also want to have the employer allow employees to 'buy up'. This can apply to upgrading a higher level MEC Plan, getting more whole-life, and especially more Aflac!

If the base MEC Plan is $74/month, but the employee wants to higher tiered level that feels a little more like traditional health insurance, having for example a $50 co-pay for a walk-in clinic, and/or wants to add family members, the difference 'can' be payroll deducted, and it can even be taken pre-tax!

Ally Health, well there's only one level anyway, and it already covers the entire household, so there is no 'buy up' there.

Transamerica, or other life carriers, certainly allow the employees to 'buy up'. Usually there's a limit to the guaranteed-issue, but with whole-life growing cash value, many times that is the only retirement vehicle these employees have.

And of course, you let them buy as much Aflac as they want!

This is actually where this gets really fun. When that employee is already getting the MEC Plan, Ally, and life insurance (with a savings component)…now you are truly a 'consultant'. You really need to present 'all' of the Aflac options so that the employee can make an informed decision. You can't take forever doing this, but a brief explanation of the accident, plus rider, hospital, cancer, dental, and vision…and even a little disability, might cost $38/week. If the employer is sponsoring $80/month as part of the 'Defined-Contribution-Package' like we just spelled out, that equates to $18.46/week paid by the company. If the employee 'wants it all', then the remaining $19.54 can be simply payroll deducted. Pre-tax, that really feels like $15/week, and that employee now has life insurance, health insurance, unlimited access to doctors without a co-pay, prescription access, a cash-building vehicle, dental, vision, accident, hospital, cancer insurance…all for $15/week! No wonder employees are so excited and thank the boss for the best benefit package ever!

But you also just doubled your projected income on the Aflac business!

'Now' what's the chance of a competitor selling voluntary insurance taking over that account?

How about "Zero"!

And you're making a lot of money!

***DISCLAIMER: Please be sure as you learn to operate as an agency that you are not suggesting that Aflac is in any way endorsing another carrier or partnering with them. Aflac's the best at what they do, but let's keep it separate. Headquarters doesn't want to risk their reputation on how well another carrier does or does not perform. Keep them separate, but be that 'agency' that brings in multiple solutions.

One last point on any time you have an employer willing to sponsor Aflac, even at any level. My first year or two in the business, I was always thrilled whenever an employer was willing to purchase the accident for every employee. Employees love it, and I made a lot of money. However I now like to position it to the employer like this, "Mr. Employer, that's really great that you're willing to sponsor a portion of this. Your employees are going to be extremely grateful for it. I would like to make one suggestion however, rather than sponsor a particular policy, might I suggest a dollar amount, like an allowance, instead? Even though you and I as business owners see the value in collecting money if you get hurt, you may have an employee that, in their own mind, would see more value in a dental policy because he is well aware that in the not-too-distant future, they are going to need to have some work done. Or another employee would jump on a hospital or disability policy because they are trying to have a baby. We want happy employees, so let's empower them to decide which policy or policies are best for them. I'll do my best to try to direct them toward the accident policy, and if they decide they want more than that, we'll have them pay the difference. They're happy, but either way you're still the hero for providing the allowance."

Now on enrollment day, to truly be a good 'benefit consultant', you need to let each employee know the different options available. The beauty is that as they listen to the different possibilities, 4 or 5 become 'maybes' in their mind. Price it all up, and human nature makes them 'want them all'. Now $38/week, less a $10/week allowance, may still be a stretch for their budget, but through the process of elimination, maybe dental can wait, and you back out a few units on the disability, and their new total is $24/week... less the $10 from the boss. That's now $14/week, pre-tax really about $9. "Is that better?" you ask.

You just doubled your premium on the case!

I caution you not to oversell, there's little worse post-enrollment than employees feeling 'buyer's remorse'. Instead, truly help that employee make a good selection, and they'll thank you. I even use phrases like, "I don't want to over-insure you", or, "I may try to talk you out of that dental policy". Being an honest salesperson goes a long way, but ironically, almost like reverse psychology, sometimes they insist that they 'want it all'. Write 'em up!

# Be the Expert

LET ME TELL YOU about my friend Scott. As a young adult, picture him with long hair, and someone who loved to ski. Well Scott got an opportunity to spend a few weeks in Vail, Colorado…and he had the time of his life. He said he skied through fresh powder snow that was several feet deep. Sometimes when he'd tumble on the slope, he'd find himself literally buried feet deep in powder, literally wondering which way was up. When that happens, you're supposed to drool a little, see which way the spit drips, and you quickly determine that the other direction must be up, and you start digging. You never get hurt because it's such soft powder. He said it was absolutely amazing!

But as his 3-week adventure was coming to a close, he started to get really depressed. He didn't want to leave. He began to wonder to himself, "How can I stay? What in the world could I do, maybe get a job around here, so that the adventure doesn't have to come to an end?"

Scott noticed an employment ad for a computer programming teacher's position at a local evening Voc-Tech school. "That's perfect" he thought, "I can ski all day and teach at night. What could be more perfect?!"

Scott pulled his hair back in a neat pony-tail, put on a nice shirt, applied for the position, (BS'ed his way through the interview),...and got it!

Awesome, right? The only problem is, Scott had never even turned on a computer in his life!

Scott literally taught himself, at least enough to stay one page ahead of the class at all times. He may have learned it the night before, but to the class seated in front of him, he was the 'expert', because he knew more than them!

He may have taken a few courses since then, but to this day Scott literally is a professional computer programmer... totally self-taught.

I tell Scott's story because all too many times, I've seen associates get overwhelmed, and freeze in their tracks, because they feel the need to 'know everything' even before they can begin. (This is especially true to all you owls out there). Well let me tell everyone out there, "No you don't!" You just need to stay '1-page ahead of the class,' like Scott did, and you are in fact the 'expert'.

As your employer presentations evolve into 'EDGE' conversations, you certainly want to lend your 'expertise' during your conversations with HRs and business owners. One way I've been able to position myself as just such an 'expert' is to offer my expertise regarding the ever-changing Affordable Care Act.

Countless times I've offered, "Our agency has familiarized ourselves with the Affordable Care Act over the last few years. Would you like the 'elevator version' of what you need to know about 'Obamacare' as an employer?" I don't think I've ever had a small employer not enthusiastically say, "Yes".

"Way back in March of 2010, Obama signed 'Obamacare' into law. Now he didn't write any of it. Honestly, I doubt he's ever read it, but he was in office, so it was named after him."

*NOTE: With the country so politically polarized as it is, we want to win them over quickly, regardless of their persuasion.*

"However, in April 2010, Obama did hire some 16,000 new IRS agents to enforce it as a tax, and that created the political firestorm we saw go back and forth for a couple years. But finally, in September of 2012, the Supreme Court finally upheld it, determined that it was Constitutional, and that it was in fact a 'tax'."

"Now the ACA is literally hundreds of pages", (and I hold my hand out to my side, charading a pile of paper about waist high), "A lot of it doesn't pertain to you unless you are a large employer, but there are 6 tenants every person really should know."

NOTE: Many HRs over the past several years have gone to multiple day-long ACA seminars, and now they're still overwhelmed with it all. If you can break it down to 6 points, you'll have them eating out of your hands. (I literally hold out 5 fingers on one hand, and just the thumb of the other).

"#1 is pre-existing conditions. Prior to healthcare reform, there were people that were uninsurable. Someone with advanced cancer might get some pain pills, but probably not that life-saving surgery. Now they can get insurance. Most people look at that as a good thing."

Next, I reiterate the smoking-clause, in case they are of an anti-Obama persuasion, we win them over by arguing that there are obvious parts that are ludicrous. However, at the same time, pro-Obama'ers feel that person with cancer receiving a life-saving surgery is the greatest thing ever.

"The only health question we can ask is, "Do you smoke cigarettes more than 3 days/week? You can smoke a carton on Thursday and Friday night while you're drinking…or smoke 'other' stuff 7 nights/week, but you'd still qualify as a non-smoker. Obviously, there are a few parts of this that might seem ludicrous, but at least that person with cancer can get insurance".

In the spirit of my entire 'You Can Too' system, we're speeding things along, told a story, and have gotten to the point, and we're already 1/6 of the way through explaining the largest bill Congress has ever passed, and honestly, they actually understand the 'pre-existing condition' clause better than after a day-long HR seminar regarding the ACA.

"#2", as I point to my middle finger, "Minimal Essential Coverage. Prior to Healthcare Reform, let's say an 18-year old landscaping guy, being all responsible and grown up, wanted to buy health insurance. He probably wouldn't buy insurance that included 'maternity' coverage. He'd have no need for it…he's a single guy. But now it doesn't matter where you buy your insurance, it has to cover all of what they've deemed 'essential'…including maternity, prescription drugs, mental health, drug and alcohol rehab etc., whether or not you'll ever use it. This is one of the main factors that has driven up premiums in the last few years. I had a case where out of 12 employees, 11 were males over 50, but because they now have to offer maternity coverage, based on their age, their premiums went up 50% in one year!"

"Truthfully, I was a huge antagonist to the whole Obamacare bill, but when the Supreme Court finally upheld it in 2012, and it was apparent that it was going to be around for a while, I reviewed my 'own' policy that day, and was shocked to find out that it did not cover cancer. I had to add it as a rider back then. But now. Since January 2014, it doesn't matter where you get your insurance, it has to cover all the 'essentials'. The thinking is this…somebody waking up in the hospital grumbling, 'Where am I. What happened?!', only to find out whatever did happen to you, 'Oh by the way, what happened to you isn't covered by your insurance'."

"#3, preventative care" (as I now point to my ring finger), it doesn't matter where you buy your insurance, all of your preventative care has to be covered 100%. It's not just your physical, but pap-smears, mammograms, flu shots, PSA checks, kids' immunizations…all available with zero out-of-pocket, no co-pays even whatsoever. Their thinking on this is that if everybody got checked every year (like we probably should), then we'd catch things much earlier. Better to find out you have stage-1 than stage-4. This would certainly save lives, but also save billions of dollars in advanced medical costs by catching things early." Sometimes I'll even add my daughter Sophie's life story (from the chapter on MEC Plans), where she has literally seized 3 engines because she never got oil changes. Yet a lot of people treat their health like that! "Don't wait until your car is smoking before you have the mechanic check it out!"

At this point we're literally ½ way through the Affordable Care Act, and it's only been a few minutes, and yet they actually understand the parts you've mentioned more so than they did after spending countless hours in seminars. And, you've proven your expertise, because they have heard 'some' of what you've explained from other ACA training to date.

"#4, the out-of-pocket-maximums. This one is actually huge," as I point to my pinkie finger. "Just a few years ago, there were a lot more foreclosures. The majority of them were linked to medical-expense bankruptcies, yet ironically, 80% of those actually 'did' have health insurance. But insurance policies used to have 'limits'. Someone might've had a million dollars' worth of coverage with Blue Cross/ Blue Shield, or 2 million with Cigna, thinking that's more insurance than they'd ever need. And honestly, Michelle and I raised 8 kids and we never came close to a million dollars of health care, even in our worst year. However, I do have a friend that was up in 'Bike Week' a few years ago, and crashed his motorcycle in Laconia. After months in the hospital and ICU, that's a several-million-dollar claim. In a case like that, Blue Cross writes a check to Concord Hospital for $1,000,000, and now they're off the hook. But then the policy holder gets a bill in the mail for the other 2 million! It might as well be a billion, they could never pay it. They feel like they've got no choice but to declare bankruptcy, and their house gets foreclosed on. However, thanks to this provision in the ACA, nobody should ever lose their house again because of medical expenses. No matter where you buy your insurance, literally the worst plan out there, has a built-in maximum. The amount creeps up a tiny bit each year, but right now the 'most' you could ever be on the hook for in a year is around $7000. About $14,000 for an entire family. Imagine if, God-forbid, all 8 of my kids ended up in ICU for months, the most I could ever owe is $14,000. You can make payments on $14,000. You can't on $4,000,000. So now, the worst insurance out there...is actually pretty good insurance. No matter where you buy it, which carrier, or how much you pay for it, it 'has' to cover all the big 'what-ifs', like cancer, mental health, maternity, drug and alcohol treatment, all your preventative is covered 100%, and the worst plan out there will protect you from bankruptcy."

"#5…the fines", pointing to my thumb, "I have my own feelings about this one. I live in New Hampshire, the 'Live Free or Die' state. We're actually the only state without a seatbelt law. Ironically, I actually do wear one, and it literally saved my life in my car accident back in 1999, but I don't think we need a law saying I 'have' to. Anyway, thanks to the current administration, this is a moot point anyway, because after January 1st, 2019, there's no longer a fine for people who don't have health insurance. Let's hope it stays that way."

## 3rd GRADE MATH

Now this is what I call 3rd grade math. Let's take a look…

If a high-deductible health plan (not even from an employer for that matter) is $400/month for an individual, with a $6000 deductible…or $700/month to have a $2000 deductible plan with co-pays, let's take a look and see how they actually compare. The difference between the two is $300/month, or $3,600/year 'more' you're paying, every year, to have the 'better' insurance, whether you ever use it or not. Odds are that 8% of the time, (or once every 12 years), you will incur a major medical expense. Now whether the full tab is $7,001 or $1,000,000, the most 'you'll' ever have to pay is $7,000 in a year.

With the high-deductible plan, you just saved $3,600/year. In ten years that's $36,000 less! Even if, Murphy's

Law, you beat the statistics and you actually had 'two' bad years in a single decade, you'd pay out $14,000 in medical expenses, and you're 'still' ahead $22,000.

And here's the other silver bullet…with a couple Aflac policies in place (like accident, cancer, and hospital), Aflac would've paid you thousands of dollars as well. You can't lose.

Now back to that conversation with that employer, "If you were to move to a HDHP, even on 10 employees you'd save well over a quarter million dollars in ten years. If we use just a portion of that savings, and say give the employees a $20/week allowance to pick out a couple Aflac policies, everyone wins, and you still save!"

We're seeing this scenario more frequently than ever!

Now back to our HCR conversation, "We still have 1 tenant left to mention, and that is that there are now several ways to purchase health insurance, where there really used to be one. You used to have to utilize a broker that would sell you a '1-size-fits-all' policy, but now you can purchase individual plans, group plans, high-deductible options, VEBAs, private exchanges, public exchanges, MEC plans…you have options."

Now one disclaimer: The MEC plan meets all the requirements except for #4, the out-of-pocket maximum, but again, if your 'house catches on fire', "Quick, go buy real insurance!"

One last tip : Using NBL (neural-body-linguistics), mention, "As health care reform evolves, you really need an expert to guide you and keep you abreast of all the necessary changes." If you ever so subtly tap your middle finger twice on your sternum, at the precise moment that the word 'expert' comes out of your mouth, that business owner and/or HR will forever rely on you for your expertise. That subtle body language is as certain as a baby kangaroo returning to his mother's pouch…and that business owner comes to you.

Now with this 6-step explanation of the 1600+ page ACA, you just accomplished what our 4-minute ER did. You're the expert, and they need you. I do encourage you to keep up with 'Benefit Pro' and other trade publications to keep abreast of the changes, but again, like my friend Scott, just stay 1-page ahead of the class.

# Urgency

AMERICANS ARE INDEED THE most impulsive shoppers on the planet. Ironically however, they hate to be 'sold'. The magic is when an informed consumer decides to make a purchase, and they think it's 'their' idea. But urgency is what gets them to pull the trigger, and 'buy now'.

Think about how many infomercials you've come across while channel surfing. In the bottom right hand corner, there's a clock counting down. Or, there's an indicator displaying 'how many are left'. And you constantly hear the phrase, "But wait, there's more!", or, "If you are one of the next ten callers, we'll throw in free shipping". Across America there's someone screaming for their wife or kid to get off the phone because, "Time's almost out," and they're about to miss a bargain. Funny thing is, it's a recorded infomercial, that I've probably seen a dozen times over the years. But they obviously still have people 'buying now', because they're still airing it.

Now as Aflac associates, we can't 'throw in a set of Ginsu knives' to get people to buy from us. And we can't give them a better price if they 'buy today' either. So how do we create the urgency?

The biggest takeaway I always use is simply making everybody aware of just how busy I am. I literally am trying to squeeze them into my demanding schedule. Now of course, we want to be fantastic servicing agents, but before the initial sale, you can't make yourself too available.

I remember enrolling a group once with a new agent named Dean. It was actually a 'town hall' meeting. Literally, Dean had gotten police, fire, highway, library, and town hall employees to all show up, I couldn't believe the turnout. The town had opted for EDB (employee direct bill), but was willing to establish the group, and obviously give us access to the town employees.

I did my usual presentation, highlighting the accident and cancer plans. Inevitably, one employee raised their hand and asked, "Do we have to sign up tonight, or can we think about it?"

My response, "Of course, there's no free set of Ginsu knives to get Aflac tonight. And the good news about Aflac is, the price will be the same when I come back next year. But if you're thinking you may want it this year, at least sit down with us for a moment. We just need to quote you a price in person, and witness a beneficiary, and we can do the rest over the phone."

Now Dean admitted later that he almost swallowed his tongue when I said, "When we come back next year...". Inside, he wanted to burst out saying, "I live in town, and I can see you whenever it's convenient for you". To his credit, he said nothing...and we enrolled every single one of them that night!

## THE 'HOLD' STRATEGY

Now when someone says, "Can I think about it?" or "Can I bring it home and talk to my wife?" You have to start with a positive affirmation. "Of course." I might even add, "I get it, I'm married too." It can't be confrontational, or you've already lost. But by 'agreeing' first, adding a little humor, and acting like you don't care, you'll have the best results.

Once you disarm them by agreeing, the only two things we need to do is 'quote you a price in person' and 'witness a beneficiary'. What does that mean? We fill out their application and they sign a PDA!

Now one of the best tools I've implemented is using the 'Hold' strategy. Downplaying the entire ordeal to the prospective policy holder, I say, "Okay, just a little 'legalese', because I put 'Hold' on this, that means you don't have Aflac until you call me. Even if you meant to call me, but didn't, you can't call me next month, after you get hurt, and try to put in a claim. Just so you understand…" This little bit of takeaway psychology, as well as my 'I don't care' attitude both contribute to the sales process.

Now in front of the prospect, I spin the PDA lengthwise, so that I can write their phone number along the perforated edge, and with my pen still hovering ask, "Okay, what's the best number to reach you at if we're playing phone tag?" Hopefully it's a cell, so we can even text. Then I continue, "Okay, today's Thursday, do you think you'll have a chance to talk to your wife over the weekend, and call me Monday? And if your wife has any questions, she can feel free to call me, I do that a lot too. And listen, if you decide not to get Aflac this year, you're not going to hurt my feelings, but if you could at least let me know either way so I can get Pam in payroll the final tally of who got what. Fair enough?"

Again, a magic way to end a sales question is "Fair enough?" How could they not agree that that's fair?

Honestly, at this stage, about 1/3 of them will just say, "You know what, never mind. Just put it through. It's only $12/week, I think I can live with that."

I 'always' say, "Are you sure?" Make them say it twice.

Of the other 2/3, almost to a science, ½ of those policy holders will be a "Yes". But had you entertained the game of 'chase' over the next week or so, you never would've captured those additional sales.

Keep it very low pressure, and an extreme (but polite) 'I really don't care if you get it or not' attitude.

2 Notes : 1) Now that most of you are using Everwell by now, remember that completed applications 'automatically' transmit once the effective date comes around, whether or not they were 'holds' in your mind. With SNG, it takes a transmittal to send, but with Everwell, be sure to 'uncomplete' those that decide to opt out before the effective date arrives. And 2) remember that Aflac is intentionally a 'Most Ethical Company in the US' (I think 11 years running). Keep that integrity going, and only transmit policies that customers want. Do the right thing…always.

Now nothing works all the time, but this 'Hold' strategy sure works an awful lot of the time. It also adds to your credibility of just how busy you are.

Another way to add urgency is at the group level. Be sure to say, "Our 'agency' is running a promotion right now for pre-schools and daycares." Just don't say 'Aflac' is running the promotion. But you can say, "Our agency is running a promotion from now 'til the end of the month, that every pre-school teacher that attends an Aflac presentation gets a free $25 Restaurant gift card.

(Again, check your state-specific allowable guidelines), just make sure that no purchase is necessary…only their attendance.

Want to add to the excitement? Raffle a door prize of an I-Pad, GoPro, or TV. Giving away something worth a sizeable dollar value gets their attention! Now is it a risk? Sure it is. But gathering the workers bees is invaluable. You'll net an advance of more than enough to cover the door prize once you enroll your first employee. (And it's another write-off).

Another 'urgency' pitch is "Our agency is offering Free EZ-Shield Identity Theft Protection for all employees of construction companies this month, just for learning how Aflac works."

Remember, this is 'your' business. Treat it like one. 'Your' initiative may be to target restaurants in June, construction companies in July, and Pre-schools in August. Just make sure you are transparent that it is the initiative of your agency, not Aflac corporate.

Urgency leads to excitement, which leads to sales.

Lastly, for your own urgency, post your own goals everywhere you can see them. I love going to DSC Tonya Manfrate's house. Posted on the front door, so she can't help but see it on the way out, a sign saying "I'm going to FAME!" On her bathroom mirror, "I'm going to Hawaii!" or wherever the next National Convention is headed.

Writing down your goals is critical. Posting them, especially where others can see them, is magic!

# The ABC's of Open Enrollment and Servicing

IN MY FIRST BOOK, I wrote about the 4 magic questions of servicing. I truly believe if we all touched our accounts every 3 months, and truly offered good service, our 'Milk Routes' will sustain us for decades to come.

But there's nothing sadder, (when it comes to servicing, or the lack thereof), than having a 'prospect' say, "I think we have Aflac actually, but I don't think anyone's seen or heard from our guy since he signed us up 5 years ago."

Dan Amos has drilled into upper management that accounts that become inactive, (have no new business written in them), for just 16 months, have a 50% chance of never being written in again!

All it takes is a billing issue or a claim that doesn't get resolved in a timely manner to make that account vulnerable. With so much competition out there, that boast that they are all 'just like Aflac', we need to fortify our accounts.

Now I have a very simple strategy that can help associates have a strategic method of servicing their book. It's called the 'ABCs of Open Enrollment'.

Joe Calarco, one of my favorite people in Aflac, actually came and taught this to my Region here in New Hampshire.

Reflecting back to the 'Milk Route' chapter, let's fast forward and assume you have 100 accounts in your book of business that you service. Now there will always be those few favorites, the accounts where HR has us meeting with new hires on a very regular, scheduled basis. Some are even so good that employees already know which policies they want, thanks to that HR being such an enthusiastic champion of Aflac.

But let's face it, we can get very 'busy' in this business. From Monday Morning Meetings to trainings, to remembering to keep your CE credits current, possibly a certification course, a scheduled benefit fair, a pre-scheduled open enrollment...not to mention at least a half dozen issues going on with either pended and/or policy holder services, each which can keep you on the phone for hours getting those issues resolved. Oh, did I mention claims assistance?

In between all that, you certainly need to make sure you respond to those clients who 'do' call us when they have a new hire for us to meet with. And, you're doing your best to prioritize time each week to meet with 10 new business owners each week, both from referrals as well as appointments set using our "You Can Too" opening line, so we can effectively continue to grow our 'milk route'. Being this busy, it's very conceivable that many accounts are getting neglected.

Now my very good friend Scott McCoy (RSC in the great state of Maine) used to be a manager for Combined Insurance. He'll tell you that when a Combined rep trips over an account that says, "We have Aflac", that probably means one of two things. Admittedly, when he'd come across a well-serviced Aflac account, you knew to just move on. Nothing can compete with that. But they were taught to ask one follow-up question, "When's the last time you saw your Aflac rep?" If the answer is "He's here every couple of months to meet with new hires, and to assist with our claims"…just walk away. But…if they answer, "Probably a year ago when they signed us up", then they would follow-up with, "Listen, Aflac's great, but they're so big that a lot of times you don't see them again. We're pretty much 'just like Aflac', but we're local, and actually a little cheaper". That's a pretty vulnerable account, that very well may succumb to a take-over.

Let's not let that be us!

Let's say you learn the hard way, and perhaps you lost an account to someone else who claimed to be 'just like Aflac'. (Now, nobody's 'just like Aflac', and after realizing that claims with any other carrier are definitely 'not' just like Aflac, they very well may come back). But let's avoid that from happening in the first place. After losing an account to a competitor, you're much more motivated to protect what you have. But where do you start? Do you just randomly start calling all 100 accounts on a Monday? Do you try to map out a course to visit them all in person? Trying to eat an elephant is overwhelming. You'll most likely make a few calls, get distracted, (or just plain busy), and that will likely just add to your frustration.

Thank you Joe for the 'ABCs of Open Enrollment'.

Here's what you do. Every quarter in the Aflac world has 13 weeks. On week one, you reach out to every account that starts with the letter A or B. That's it. From 'Al's Roofing' to 'Affordable Car Care', to 'Billy's Diner' to 'Bedford Tool & Die'.

Whether you have 5 accounts or 105, just reach out to the As and Bs in week 1.

Week 2…call every account that starts with C or D.

Week 3…the Es and Fs.

There are 26 letters in the alphabet, and 13 weeks in a quarter. 2 'letters' each week, and you've touched every account every 3 months…4 times/year.

What works out really well is that we all know how crazy busy the last few weeks are every quarter (Power Weeks). But thankfully, there aren't a whole lot of accounts that start with the letters X, Y, or Z. Week 11 is actually U and V. Week 12 is W and X. Week 13…Y and Z. It works out perfect.

I recommend that out of 4 touches/year, 2 should be in person. I also recommend that early on in your relationship with that account that you 'condition' them to expect to hear from you every 3 months. This way also, if an issue does arrive, such as some kind of billing frustration, (which we all know do come up from time to time), in the back of their mind they at least know if they never get around to calling you first, at least they are assured that before too long, you'll be checking in with them anyway.

I'm telling you, it works!

A quick reminder of the 4 magic servicing questions:

1.  Any Billing Issues?

2.  Any Claims Issues?

3.  Have any employees terminated?

4.  Any New Hires?

Now of course what we really want to know is #4. 'Are there any new hires to write?' But going right for that is like trying to kiss that girl on the way 'to' the restaurant on the first date LOL. Let's ask all 4, address any issues necessary, and 'then' kiss the girl. Then you'll continuously be writing that new hairstylist, mechanic, or dishwasher.

However, I'd like to expand on #3 a little more.

When you ask her, "Has anyone left your employ recently?", actually take notes. Jot down the names, and reach out to those parting employees. Of course you're already looking forward to selling Aflac to their replacement and make another sale, but let's also protect your renewals on the back end by reaching out to that employee.

For starters, especially when you offer some assistance, that employee just may want to keep that accident policy if it is still available at $6/week. Remind them that wherever they worked, they were getting a significant discount. By reminding them of the value, many will continue some or all of their coverage, on a direct basis.

Granted, Headquarters would've eventually sent them a computer-generated letter offering continuing coverage, but many times it may simply appear to be junk mail and never get opened…or even if they meant to, if they simply 'got busy' and never got around to filling it out, that policy goes away. On top of that, by the time they do get around to doing it, they very well may owe two months of premium, which could be harder for them to swing, especially if they are currently unemployed.

But even more valuable is saying to that parting employee, "Where are you going to be working now? Perhaps we can just have your new employer take it out of your paycheck there". If they are already an Aflac account, it's real simple, even if it's somebody else's account. However, it's much more likely that it is not an account yet, and that could very well lead you to opening a separate, brand new account.

The other option, if that employee doesn't yet have another job lined up say, "Hey I can't promise you anything, but I know Aflac's looking for a couple people right now. Let me see if I can get you an interview." Nominate them!

That is exactly what I did with Mandi Manoogian. She had worked for an Aflac customer of ours, a restaurant in Portsmouth, NH. When she was leaving, I was helping her 'port' her policies, but I also asked her, "Have you ever considered sales?" She really hadn't, but she agreed to meet with me, and the rest is history. She was teachable from the start, but she drank the Kool-aid, from writing down her goals to visualizing her desired outcomes. In a little over 2 years, she's not only taken multiple free trips with Aflac to destinations like the Dominican Republic and Cabo, Mexico, she actually in training to become a DSC. She's already had at least one month where she earned over $25,000, and is currently the #1 top account opener, not just within the Region, but the entire 3-state Market!

I'm sure glad I asked her!

Back to the open-enrollment conversations we have with our clients quarterly. Condition them to expect your call every 3 months, and even expect that every 'other' quarterly check-in will be an in-person visit. If not much has changed, then the in-person visit is mostly exchanging pleasantries, small talk, and rapport building. Bring coffee, and remember (or write down a cheat note in their file), remembering how they take it. If an issue does arise, then you're there to fix it. But this semi-annual in-person meeting also makes you aware of any changes the company is experiencing. Perhaps they've just had to move to a High

Deductible Health Plan to save money. Isn't that something you'd like to know sooner than later? We can definitely help with that! Maybe you were unaware that they just opened a second location. Perhaps dental and vision have been talked about recently. There's 'always' a new strategy, initiative, value-added service, additional carrier that you can suggest.

You'll be in the right place at the right time!

What I desire is an account that has me on speed-dial, that feels they have direct access to me, multiple lines of business in place, value-added services that I perform on a regular basis, possibly even an additional carrier as well (like Ally Health). Now I envision my presence in that account as an impenetrable castle, surrounded by a moat full of hungry alligators, a draw-bridge, and buckets of hot tar positioned on top of the wall.

Now when a competitor hears, "We have Aflac", they're not going anywhere!

# Brokers

Now some veteran agents, like Jim Gregory of northern Vermont (who's a President's Club recipient and often writes in excess of $400,000 to $500,000/year), will tell you, "Brokers suck!"

Other seasoned Aflac reps, like Steve Karas of Massachusetts who wrote over $300,000 in a single case thanks to a cooperated effort with the broker channel will tell you, "You 'have' to work with brokers".

Honestly, these two extremes can agree to disagree, but the reality is that brokers, especially in this post-Obamacare climate, have absolutely invaded our space. Really, it's been out of necessity. Thanks to the 'Affordable' Care Act, brokers have lost HUGE income streams, and have been forced to migrate 'down-market', which is in our space. They've got to find ways to make up for all of that lost revenue.

Now to their credit, many Aflac agents embraced the broker-partner model, even long before the ACA was a thing. But for the most part, the DNA of the average Aflac rep was that we were in competition 'against' brokers in most situations. Associates looked at brokers primarily as someone who cuts out 30% of their commissions, usually without doing a whole lot.

Well, like I stated in a previous chapter, change is inevitable. You can either fight it (like Blockbuster did), or capitalize on it. If you merely insist on digging in your heels, allow me to explain what 'could' happen.

In my first book, I shared a success story of how in my fifth month as an Aflac associate, I made in excess (in my pocket), over $8000 in a week when I enrolled a particular RV dealership here in New Hampshire. Shortly after, I enrolled their other location, about an hour away. Soon after that, I learned that they had another location in Cape Cod, so I got my Massachusetts license, and I enrolled them too…and the cash register was chirping!

Soon after, I learned of their location in central Florida, so I said, "Kids, we're going to Disney World!" We camped at Fort Wilderness for the week, exploring the different theme parks each day, but I went out for one day, and enrolled the dealership, made almost $2,000, and wrote off the trip as an expense! This business got awesome quick.

Over the next few years, the RV company continued to acquire dealerships in Pennsylvania, Virginia, Connecticut and Georgia. I did employ the aid of agents in other states (that I'd either come to know on my previous book/ speaking tours, or came to know from multiple Convention and FAME trips). I believe I was up to 10 locations enrolled. They were an endless stream of new hires to write throughout the year, especially during their peak season.

Then came my first wake up call to 'brokers'.

Totally out of the blue, I received an e-mail that simply informed me that their new 'health broker', who had just taken over writing the health insurance for the entire company, was offering them a 15% discount on their health insurance…if they dropped all the Aflac! Their health carrier apparently offered coverage that was 'just like Aflac', only a little cheaper, and a single invoice would make so much more sense anyway…

"Are You Kidding Me?!"

Thankfully, after an exhaustive effort by my administrator and myself, an awful lot of the employees did 'port' their Aflac policies, transitioning over to employee-direct-bill. But even more of them didn't. And there goes the biggest stop on my milk route…

Now is that other company 'Just like Aflac'? Of course not. Is it possible that I may win that company back in the future? Sure. But it was still a tremendous wake-up call to the new 'Post-Obamacare/Brokers-in-our-Space' world we now live in.

But let's totally switch gears for a second.

Let's not think about brokers at all for a moment, but rather go back to what it takes to organically add stops to our 'milk routes'. So what are the different steps?

1. Probably planning an area we are going to target

2. Canvassing…making those decision maker introductions (and/or dialog to set up an appointment

3. Running the decision maker appointment

4. Establishing enrollment conditions/setting up the employee meeting

5. Presenting to the employees

6. Enrolling (hopefully same day)

7. "Getting Paid"

8. And then the back-office post-enrollment stuff, like PDAS, deduction summaries, pended business…all the way to 1st invoice review

Of those 8 steps…which one(s) would you say take the most time and effort? Which are your favorite parts?

Most would agree that the majority of our efforts are spent making those introductions and setting those appointments. It's the most essential and most important part.

Now let me ask you, if someone else was willing to knock on all the doors, pitch those businesses, and set the table for quality employer presentations, what would that be worth?

Many associates in fact do pay literally hundreds of dollars to appointment setting companies to do just that… get the decision makers to the table.

Again, let me ask you, if you were handed a teed up company, then you ran the DM meeting, and subsequently wrote $10,000 AP days later with little effort…would it be worth paying (splitting in) that associate who got you that appointment in the first place? Of course it would.

Yet if you really think about it, that's exactly what employing/partnering with a broker can look like.

You see, brokers already have a book-of-business, of typically between 50 and 200 clients. They 'already' have a relationship with those accounts and HRs, and furthermore are seen by those companies as their 'trusted benefit advisor'.

Now what if their 'trusted advisor', advises them to do Aflac? Why 'wouldn't' that warrant that 30% (or 40%) to be paid to that broker? If the table's been set, and you can simply slip in at 'showtime', then you can simply do what you love to do best…present and enroll.

Truthfully, brokers 'are' typically absolute control freaks. But really, they have to be. Their relationship with each client is literally worth thousands of dollars. But once that broker sees you in action, and comes to appreciate all you truly have to offer, many will quite literally open their book to you. I even have a couple associates in my region that literally have offices set up within a broker's office, with absolute cart-blanch access to their book.

That my friend is a gold mine. Just always keep in mind that you are representing that broker, not merely yourself, when you are with their clients.

Now you better not be a fly-by-night agent who merely looks to write business, never to be seen again. This is where you get a chance to shine even further as you deliver rock-star back office support as well. If you don't deliver on the back end as well, they'll drop you like a hot potato. But over time, showcase your abilities, and continue to earn their confidence, and that relationship can pay you dividends for decades.

Does every broker partnership work out? Definitely not. Some are quite adversarial, and perhaps will never play well in the same sandbox. So what. Yet, educating yourself on the whole broker opportunity can be priceless.

We as Aflac have some distinct advantages as well. For starters, we experience 'level renewals for life', that cannot be BOR'd (with the exception of Group). To really comprehend this, walk through the following scenario with me...

Let's say a local mom & pop broker actually does offer incredible service to a particular account. Perhaps (unlike most) they actually have relationships with many of the rank & file employees, visit on-site often, and they are more than thorough each year at open enrollment, and don't just rely on that HR to collect all the paper health apps. Thanks to their exhaustive efforts, the employees actually understand and appreciate their benefits after very informative benefit meetings. That health case may earn that broker a significant income, but good for him. They've worked hard and they deserve those hard-earned renewals.

But now picture this…months later a larger broker is systematically acquiring many local brokers, and establishing a heavy presence in the community. Let's say that broker over time starts to buddy up with the business owner, and routinely treats him to rounds of golf. Then one day, between the 7th green and the tee on hole number eight, that broker brings up the subject and asks that business owner for a BOR (broker-of-record letter). The business owner obliges, not knowing exactly what it means perhaps, but just like that…all of those hard-earned renewals from that 1st broker, will from now be deposited into broker #2's checking account! Just—like—that.

Sound cut-throat? Of course, but that happens every day. Furthermore, that new larger broker, who probably has a bigger expense account, might also start to send that HR lady to a bed & breakfast in Cape Cod every summer. Oh yeah…that happens too.

If this whole scenario is new to you, you may at least start to appreciate why brokers aren't usually the most trusting people.

When that BOR arrives, that broker might assume that they will also be inheriting your Aflac renewals. Here's the good news…they don't. Thankfully your Aflac renewals are protected. But it still may be the end of you ever writing a new hire in that account.

Other times, brokers intend to have you continue to do what you do, but moving forward, split them in at 40%. Unfortunately, that's the world we live in.

However, like the old adage says, "If you can't beat 'em, join 'em!"

Next time that does happen to you (you get notified of the BOR), how about reaching out to that broker. Start developing a relationship, bring 'em to lunch. Invite them to actually come and see you in action. Perhaps they'll be truly impressed, and it will result in a future partnership, attacking the rest of their book.

If and when this happens, do stand your ground and remember that you truly have a lot to offer. For starters, most brokers don't actually have the boots-on-the-ground to conduct sizeable enrollments. Perhaps until now they've had to employ per diem enrollment services. You (along with the other agents on your district or regional team) are equipped to perform that incredible service. In fact the Aflac sales force has literally become the largest enrollment firm in America.

Also, whether it's carrier partners you can bring to the table, or value-added-services like dependent audits and beneficiary updates…you have an enormous amount of additional value that you can bring to the table.

Now I'm am really going to hurt your brain for a moment. What if, in an already successful account, where you've never heard a word about their broker, you actually get proactive, and 'ask' for their current health broker's information. You could literally pursue 'them'. I'd even recommend inviting them to meet with you, and even offer the following, "Mr. Broker, I'd actually like to offer including you on this case, and offer you a split of the commission, on the one condition that you actually attend the enrollment, in person, and see first hand what I have to offer. Then, if I've truly impressed you, you see first hand what we do, and witness for yourself the overwhelming reception we get from the employees…then we meet post-enrollment, and if I've truly impressed you, then we can talk about possibly offering the same benefits to your existing book."

You are quite literally offering them revenue, that fell in their lap. But that could also be the start of something great.

By the way, what percentage of your accounts that have W-2 employees do you think actually have a broker? You might not realize this, but it's close to 100%. Even if they are a small company that doesn't offer health insurance, they 'have' to purchase Worker's Comp, and that requires a broker. It may very well be a P & C (property and casualty) broker, that may not even have a health license, but why not approach 'them' with the novel idea of offering Aflac to their existing book?

Brokers are always looking to generate additional lines of income.

In fact, here in NH, Marie is a rock-star agent that has written two hospitals...through a P & C broker!

Listen, I get that not everyone exactly embraces the broker concept, but you at least need to be informed, so that you can continue to thrive in today's marketplace.

And if you ever envision someday enrolling giant school systems and 500-life manufacturing companies, and you think you'll ever be able to do so without partnering with a broker, you are simply being naïve.

Yet, by writing dozens of pizza shops, diners, hair salons and garages, you'll surely hone your skills to the point that you'll be more than qualified to 'showcase' yourself to brokers in the larger market.

And lastly, we now possess a wealth of support to brokers. With the assistance of Aflac's relatively new corporate broker channel, we can fully implement strategies like core-enrollment. You truly have an edge. The landscape is more competitive than ever, and the market is ripe. With literally half of the brokers out there still enrolling their health cases on paper apps, conditions couldn't be better. It's time to make your presence known, and become invaluable to them.

Embrace change, and capitalize on it!

# How Great is This Opportunity?

I ALREADY SHARED AN "Aha" moment I experienced in an earlier chapter, when I shared what an impact helping somebody 'not' lose their house had on me.

Now allow me to share with you the other big "Aha" moment I experienced pretty early on in my career that helped me to realize just how blessed we are as Aflac agents.

I had just developed the 'lunch & learn' strategy for dental offices. Possibly 2 ½ years into my business, and I thought the same lunch & learn approach might be perfect for my own chiropractor's office.

Indeed, after a couple of pizzas and a salad, the staff of about 5 female therapists, assistants, and office workers had all enrolled in at least the accident policy. I was able to upsell a couple dental and sickness policies as well.

After the staff began to return to their work stations, the last person to enroll was the doctor himself. Of course, whether a dentist or chiropractor, if you don't have full use of your hands, you're not practicing medicine, so I recommended a short-term disability policy for him.

Usually, I suggest a benefit amount that will at least cover their largest expense for a year. Almost scripted, I asked, "So Dr. Andy, what's your biggest expense, probably your mortgage?"

Without hesitating he said, "No way, my school loans!" Now he and his wife are both chiropractors, and share a practice, but 10 years out of medical school, his school loans were still over $2800/month!

I also had to ask him for his annual income, so that I could determine what level of benefit he was eligible for.

Then it hit me, just 3 years into the business, I was not only making more than my doctor was, but he was still being haunted by a mountain of college debt and I wasn't. He was also (and still is) married to his practice, and had to be in his office at least 4 days/week, from 10:00am until at least 6:00. And there's no way he could 'ever' vacation 6 to 8 times/year!

Now like I mentioned in my first book, if in your heart of hearts, you were born to be a doctor, then you shouldn't do anything else. But otherwise, if you have big dreams, I hope you realize just what a great opportunity you have as an independent Aflac agent.

Now, let's compare how the Aflac opportunity is also head and shoulders above similar opportunities, with other carriers.

Almost a decade ago, when I first began to explore the insurance industry as a career path, I actually met with 'two' companies…Aflac and New York Life.

Now knowing what I know now, there are a lot of reasons I am glad I chose Aflac over NY Life, but at the time, the determining factor was primarily that the life insurance sales model was typically targeting individuals, which means you are at their kitchen table…mostly on nights and weekends, because that's when they're home, since during the day they are at work.

Well I determined that I was tired of working nights and weekends. I wanted to be at 'my' kitchen table on nights and weekends, not someone else's. With Aflac, you're primarily talking to business owners during business hours, and enrolling their employees during the workday.

That's definitely more of what I was looking for.

Now New York Life is a fantastic company. They are financially strong, have had a terrific reputation for close to a century, and I met some really great people there. But I recently learned that with NY Life, they have something called 20-year 'cliff-vesting'. Simply put, that means if you worked for them for 19 years, and stopped, your renewals disappear before long.

With Aflac, I believe you're 50% vested in just a year! That's a much more attractive business plan for someone starting a career with insurance.

Just don't take this opportunity for granted. If you emptied your savings, borrowed from your in-laws, and put your house up as collateral, to purchase a Dunkin' Donuts franchise for $300,000, would you ever consider giving up after a 'bad day'? Of course not!

If you treat your Aflac business 'as if' you had invested significant capital in it, you'll be 'All IN', and you're guaranteed success.

Recently our Market Director Mike Chille gave us his take on how there are really 3 ways to look at the Aflac opportunity. It can be a 'sales job', a career, or your own business.

#1) As a sales job, honestly Aflac's not all that great. If someone just wants to make $100,000/year, and you possess some sales skills, go sell cars. You may have to give up your nights and weekends but that's about it. You'd probably get at least some sort of 'draw', and maybe even some health insurance. With Aflac, as a sales job, there's no base pay, no traditional benefits, and it can take a few weeks to actually get your activity going. On the surface, side by side, Aflac's not necessarily the best 'sales job'.

#2) Now as a career path, you can realize that in a relatively short period of time, you can potentially build a substantial income, and your renewals can become quite significant over time. There's plenty of room for advancement, and the potential is literally unlimited.

#3) But as a 'business owner', it's a gold mine. Like a franchise, you have the huge advantage of a brand name, and in our case the #1 brand in America! You have the huge tax advantages of being self-employed, but without the overhead!

If starting an Aflac business actually 'did' cost $300,000, it'd still be worth it, but it doesn't. Yet, if you act as if it did, don't take the brand recognition for granted, and you do take advantage of all the leadership support, put systems in place, and put into practice everything laid out in the book you're holding…you'll realize just how blessed you are to be representing the greatest brand in the greatest country on the planet, at the most opportune time in history.

Your future's so bright, you probably want to invest in some sunglasses!

# The Millionaire Mindset

WANT TO HEAR A sad fact? 96% of lottery winners are literally bankrupt within 2 years!

That's incredible isn't it? But why?

Success is not just accumulating wealth, it's much more than that. It's also keeping that wealth, multiplying it, and making an impact with it.

Windfall millionaires usually lose it all because they don't change their thinking. There is actually a money consciousness that you need to develop. Some, (many in fact), don't feel worthy of riches, because of negative programming they heard growing up, like, "The rich get richer and the poor get poorer", as well as associating with the term 'filthy rich'…where did that come from?

For some people, their current friends are usually in a very similar income bracket. So if that person, let's say suddenly triples their income…they actually feel awkward (and undeserving) when they spend time with those same friends.

This is all unfortunate, because they are all a product of the way people think.

Looking back at history, Abraham (the father of the Muslim, Jewish, and Christian faiths) was the wealthiest man of his day. King Solomon was arguably the richest man that has ever lived. Yet both of these men did incredibly good things with their money. Say what you will about his politics, (I happen to be a huge fan), and his Tweets, but Donald Trump gives millions and millions of dollars to charity every year. He couldn't do that if he wasn't wealthy.

So the real quest is not merely accumulating wealth, but proving to be a good steward of it once you've arrived.

Let's fast forward, and take a ride into the not too distant future. What does retirement look like for you? What's the magic number (dollar value) that you'll have to have accumulated to determine that you've arrived? Is it a million dollars?

Let's just use that number and see what life would/could look like once you've arrived, and accumulated a net worth of 1 million dollars. Envision $1,000,000 liquid, cash, in the bank.

What you 'don't' want is to just visualize a dwindling balance in your checking account. You don't simply purchase a $60,000 sports car, and now have a balance of $940,000. Then $400 on a fancy dinner in the city, and now you're at $939,600. Like 'hundreds' of NBA players who've gone broke really fast...your money will be gone!

Instead, let's take say $300,000 of it and do something really cool. Let's buy a 4-family apartment building. We'll own the building outright, so there's no mortgage payments. Of course there are property taxes and insurance, and eventually some normal wear and tear repairs. But let's picture our 4 tenants each paying $1000/month rent. That's $4000/month, or a $48,000/year return on our

$300,000 investment. Let's be real though and factor in a 15% vacancy allowance. Now less $7200, we're still over $40,000/year. Let's even give taxes, insurance, and repair costs another $10,000...that's 'still' $30,000/year positive cash flow. Let's even pay a property management company $3000, so none of the tenants ever know we own the building. That's 'still' a $27,000 net gain, or 9% on your money! Your $300,000 is still safe because you own the building outright, yet that's still a 9% return, every year... ummm, way better than money sitting in the bank! And your balance (million dollar net worth) isn't dwindling like that NBA player. You're 'still' a millionaire...but now with an additional $3000/month cash flow.

That's not all. Here's where the magic really starts to happen. That building you just purchased for $300,000 will most likely be worth $315,000 a year from now. That's because historically, real estate has risen in value approximately 5% each year. There are certainly highs and lows, but the 'only' way to actually lose money in real estate, is if you are forced to sell when property values are down. As long as you ride it out, you'll always be able to sell it at a profit...every time. Let me give you an example. My parents bought my childhood home for $16,900, just before I was born. Before I turned 40, my parents sold that property, and just the land sold for over a quarter million dollars! Now you can be sure that they rode out several roller-coaster economic ups and downs over a couple decades, but even still, that property will 'never' sell for $16,900 again. Not even close.

So in reality, back to our $300,000 purchase of that apartment building, we actually need to add another $15,000 gain to our profits. Now you're at $42,000/year, which is a 14% return. 'Way' better than money just sitting in the bank. (And you're not even the landlord, you have someone else collect the rents, fill the vacancies, and answer the phone at 2:00am when a pipe is leaking...you just collect the profits!)

But are you ready to REALLY start thinking like a millionaire?

Let's incorporate the 'OPM' principle (other peoples' money), the real secret of enormous wealth.

Let's take that same $300,000, and instead of buying that one property outright, let's buy 4! By putting $75,000 (25%) down on each property, you still avoid having to pay mortgage insurance. Sure, there's a small mortgage (probably around $1500/month) on each property, but your net rents are now $32,000/month (after a 15% vacancy allowance). Let's figure $6000 for the mortgages, you're still netting $6400/month, or $77,000/year. Even after you pay the management company, taxes and insurance, that's still at least $60,000/year of pure profit, or $5000/month!

Better still, 'each' building went up $15,000 in value, so a year later your 1 million dollar net worth has 'grown' to $1,060,000...'and' you have another $5000/month coming in for life.

What if you did that 2 more times (Buying 12 buildings, $75,000 down on each one, investing $900,000)?

Now you have over $200,000/year coming in, and you still have $100,000 in the bank (or a coffee can) somewhere as a security blanket...but your net worth grows by $180,000/year!

In just 6 years, you could sell all those buildings, and now you'd have over $2,000,000!

I teach this very concept in my 'Kaizen' class, which is mostly comprised of brand new Aflac agents...most with 'no' money in the bank. They are not currently in the position to wonder, "How should I invest a million dollars?" Most are starting at zero, (or possibly even far below zero), just like I was 9 ½ years ago. Some are literally young kids just out of school, and this is in fact their first career ever.

So why worry about how to invest a million dollars before you have it? Simply, so you don't blow it when you do get there. And by planning what you'll do when you get there, you actually adjust your mindset to ensure you actually do get there in the first place.

Joel Osteen recently shared a story of when he was a guest in an extremely successful actor's home, who is also now producing his own movies. He couldn't help but notice an entire wall plastered with index cards. Joel had to ask what they were, and he explained how he was currently working on the script for a new film, and each index card represented a scene.

Seeming to represent an overwhelming proposition, Joel asked, "How in the world do you know where to start?"

"That's easy", he told him, "Often you start with the end of the movie, and you shoot the final scene, before the rest of the film is even written. Then you work backwards."

You have to know your destination first, and then you figure out how to get there. If you don't have a specific destination, 'any' road will get you there.

That's why, back to your '100 life goals', go figure out what you want...then you start on the journey. Then, you begin your quest of acquiring your million dollar net worth...one door at a time, one account at a time.

That's why you 'have' to develop the millionaire mindset.

And that's why I teach even the newest associates in my Kaizen class the '10/10/10 principle'.

For starters, I teach that whether you make $2000 this month, or $102,000, you take 10% and give it away to charity. I believe this with everything in me.

One of my life goals is to sponsor 100 World Vision Kids. My wife and I have a collage of the kids we sponsor. (We don't have 100 yet, but I can't wait to cross off that goal)! Think about it, at just $35/month per sponsored child, that means it only costs $42,000/year to keep 100 kids alive on the other side of the world! You can do a lot wrong with your life, but you just made the world a better place because you were in it. That's why my wife and I support a sex-trafficking safe house for girls in Florida, a food ministry in Manchester, NH, our local church, the Aflac Cancer Center, and countless other ministries including supporting my missionary niece in Nepal. We give more to church and charity each year than the average American makes.

Now here's the cool part. It's not why you do it, but it comes back to you 10-fold. It's the craziest thing! You don't have to believe in gravity, but if you jump off your hotel balcony, you're going to go down. It's the same with giving. If you're not sure who to give to, I recommend you start with your local church or synagogue. The network of churches across America collectively feeds many millions of people every day, both in our own communities and around the world. Maybe you're passionate about an environmental issue, or an animal rescue…just do it!

And you 'start' with giving, the second you get paid. You don't wait and see if there will be extra left over at the end of the month. You and I both know it will never work like that.

I remember where my old office used to be in Manchester, NH, I could literally see the Jewish Synagogue from my window. When I lived in the north end of Manchester, my youngest daughter Cady, who went to Hillside school, was invited to a classmate's Barmitzvah celebration. From what I recall, this sixth grader's present that day was something like $60,000 in an envelope! I happen to know the founder of this area's Cardiac Hospital, other doctors, high profile attorneys, pilots, famous business owners and entrepreneurs, who are all members there. My former pastor Steve (who was brought up with a Christian mother and a Jewish father) said his dad was also a member, and the ironic thing is that it wasn't even a choice. He said if you were a member there, they automatically deducted 10% of your 1099 or W-2! But guess what, every single member there that I know is extremely wealthy. They are all in fact millionaires. Collectively, that church feeds thousands, if not a million, people a day. Again, it's not 'why' they do it, but 'because' they do it, it comes back to them tenfold… literally.

So again, the first principle of the '10/10/10', is take the first 10% you earn, and make your world a better place because you're in it, and give it away.

Next, take a second 10% and 'plant it'. You take 10%, and you invest it into things that will make money for you while you're sleeping. So I talk with my agents about everything from stocks, to options, to Universal Indexes, and of course real estate. Did you know that McDonald's makes more money on real estate than it does on hamburgers? McDonald's Holding company bought countless city blocks across America, and in fact many of their competitors (including Burger King) actually lease their property, in one form or another, from McDonald's! That's why I personally own rental property. I rent out parking spaces in a downtown city lot, where I do really well, especially during snow emergencies. I own storage units that I rent out, and I bought a lake house up north that has become a significant rental income stream as well.

I shared with my Kaizen class recently how a little over a year and a half ago, I cashed in $67,000 of my Aflac stock, and put it down on a 3-family apartment building in Manchester. The 2 apartments upstairs cover the small mortgage, so the downstairs tenant that pays $300 every week like clockwork is just another stream of passive income for me. And…I purchased the building for $270,000, but in less than 2 years it has gone up in value and is now worth about $310,000. When I was on vacation a few weeks ago, visiting my daughter Kirstie in Texas, I actually made $9000 that week. Of course a lot of that was Aflac money and renewals, but I have additional vehicles in place so that my money grows while I'm working, playing, on vacation, or sleeping. My 'net worth' grows significantly every month. (Remember, I was flat broke less than 10 years ago when I came to this great Aflac opportunity).

But that's another reason that I incorporate other carriers as well. Even though they are primarily an 'AIS Factor' for me to set the table for writing Aflac, and that is by far where you will indeed make the most money, yet I've increased my income by thousands more a month as well.

Now I read a lot, mostly books written by multi-millionaires, to learn their mindset. (I've actually already read 6 books in the first 4 months this year). But a prevailing theme is that the average multi-millionaire actually has 8 lines of income.

I believe that Aflac will always be your most significant source of income, and by committing a significant portion of those dollars (and money from your Aflac stocks), your wealth will continue to outlive you by generations.

I also shared with my Kaizen class a check for $157,000 that I walked away from a closing with, after owning a property for just under 5 years.

When I speak in front of either crowds or classrooms, teaching the 'Millionaire Mindset', I equate the second 10% (saving/investing) to corn.

Let's say at the beginning of every month, you got a delivery of corn dropped off, a rather large bushel in fact. As soon as that delivery arrives, you immediately start feasting on your corn. You can make tortillas, nachos, cornmeal, corn muffins, corn chowder, and some wicked good cornbread. You can have yourself a Corn Fiesta! But come the end of the month, your supply starts to wind down, and you start to run out of corn. Anxiously, you await the first of the month, and your next big bushel of corn to arrive.

But what if you took just 10% of those corn kernels, and planted them in the ground? What would happen? Granted, you might have a little less corn to Fiesta with, and nothing would immediately happen. But...after just a few weeks, you'd notice a few sprouts poking their way through the topsoil. Before long, those sprouts grow into giant stalks, each yielding countless ears, which each supply hundreds of new kernels. Before long, you'd have more corn than you could possibly eat. You could sell a whole lot of it. In fact, you could take 10% and donate it to a food pantry, take another 10% of the corn and start a whole new crop in another cornfield, and make a fortune selling the fruits of your labor, and still have more corn than you could possibly eat in a lifetime!

But so many people eat all of their corn, and it's stupid.

And, just like the first 10 % (giving), you never wait until the end of the month and see what's 'left' to invest. We've already been there, and there won't be anything to invest. You have to do it first, at the beginning of the month, every single time.

Now for the final 1/3 of my '10/10/10 Principle'. (This I learned from another multi-millionaire Harv Eker), you take 10%, and you absolutely blow it! The first two (giving and saving) certainly take discipline in order to stay the course. But if you don't reward yourself, even along the way, you just might start to resent the first two. That's why every once in a while you spend hundreds of dollars on a new dress for your wife, go treat yourself to a $300 dinner at that fancy steakhouse restaurant, and get away to that cute little Bed & Breakfast every once in a while. Live a little. Don't wait until you 'arrive' to start enjoying life, going through the motions like a stingy jerk. Life's too short for that! Carefully measure 10% of your 'splurge fund', save it up, and take a cruise!

But after the 10/10/10…you learn to live on the other 70%, whatever that is, because you can. You live within your means. You don't buy things on credit that you have no business purchasing yet. You don't buy a car you can't afford, just to impress your neighbors. (They don't like you anyway!) You attack any debt you do have with a vengeance. You even make adjustments, if necessary, if you are 'mortgage broke', or are otherwise living out of balance.

Be a good steward now, and the lifestyle of your dreams will soon follow.

But if you live by these principles… give 10%, save and invest 10%, and blow 10% on yourself, and then learn to live within your means on the other 70%, you're guaranteed to become a millionaire. As soon as possible you start by purchasing a home, instead of paying rent your whole life, and over time increase your portfolio. (Two of my kids have purchased their first homes within the last few months!) You will be creating real lasting wealth that will indeed outlive you by generations. You could be a school janitor and live by the 10/10/10 Principle, and you'll eventually become wealthy. You're just bound to get there a whole lot faster thanks to the significant income potential within the Aflac opportunity.

Last year, my wife and I's "Splurge 10" was to take 40+ people on a cruise. We took parents, kids, and grandkids. All my management team (my DSCs) got to go, my administrative staff, as well as my top producing and account opening associates. We paid for an open bar for the week, and even covered gratuities on an all-out all-inclusive 7-night cruise to Bermuda. (It was awesome, so awesome that my assistant Allie's husband gained 14 pounds in just one week!) Everyone lived like kings and queens on the high seas.

John Emond, one of my DSCS, and his wife Jillian, who is also a superstar writing agent, also qualified as an associate, so we invited them to even bring their son and parents. But on the cruise, admittedly John drank his fair share of free wine during the art auction. We saw them later that night, and he laughed and said, "I think I just spent

2-months' worth of my 'blow 10%' in an hour!" Apparently he bought a lot of art! LOL

It gets better. A couple weeks after the cruise, Norwegian Cruise Line must have assumed that John was some kind of art aficionado, because he received a private invitation to an exclusive art auction at the Ritz Carlton in Boston a few weeks later. He actually went…and bought another one!

Now buying art had never been on his radar prior to the cruise, but now he insists that it's kind of both, a splurge 10% 'and' an invest 10% at the same time, because apparently art increases in value over time. Whatever, but John and Jill are certainly living life to the fullest!

When I met John and Jill, I'm guessing 7 or 8 years ago now, they were actually in pretty dire straits. In fact, at the time they were very much in danger of losing their home.

Now fast forward to 2018. Not only were they able to save their home, but that is now their office! My wife and I recently visited John and Jill to see and celebrate their closing on a beautiful 62-acre log cabin estate they recently purchased and now call home!

Thankfully, on faith at first, they embraced my '10/10/10', and took it to heart. They are certainly living large, and enjoying life to the fullest. At the same time they are saving and investing (from art to real estate), and indeed have multiple streams of income, but John confided in me that the most impactful realization came when he filed his taxes earlier this year, and realized just how much they had been able to give to church and charity last year…as much as many people make in a year! Because they live by those principles, this world is indeed a better place because they're in it. Great job guys!

Over 100 pages ago, I challenged you to write down your 100 life goals. If you didn't do it then, please do it now.

Decide what you want your 'final scene' to look like. Then work backwards.

I'll say it one more time, "Think big...REALLY BIG!"

# You're 'Still' Not Alone

*"Are you the author of the book "You Can Too'? I just finished reading the 'You are not alone' chapter, and I feel like you were writing directly to me"*

—*Tara G.*

IN MY FIRST BOOK, I included a chapter called, "You're Not Alone". In it I explained how faith played a huge part in my success. It still does.

Reiterating my first volume, I still hate religion, but I love to seek God and glorify Him with all my heart. It is definitely 'not' the same thing.

Allow me to share another story from years past that helped cement my faith. If I've spoken at your Market's Kick-off over the years, there's probably a good chance you've heard this one.

During the period of time (in my prior life), when I was literally bringing 5 kids to work with me every day as a self-employed delivery driver in the greater Boston area, I was grateful that God had orchestrated my path in such a way that I found myself in the 'only' career that a father of 5 could literally bring his small children to work every day.

But it was still tough, and I was definitely 'existing', living week to week.

My right canine (eye) tooth had a huge hole developing in it. It was actually unsightly to look at if I smiled too big. But major dental work was the 'last' priority in my budget. I was literally struggling just to keep the lights on.

I was tired of seeing it, and I was in fact fed up. Now what I did next might seem a little 'far out' to you, but I said a 'Prayer of Faith'. It sounded something like this, "God, I've got so much on my freaking plate right now...I need you to heal my tooth please. In Jesus name, amen!"

That was it. Now the 'only' person I told was my mom, because she's definitely a prayer person, but everybody else wouldn't simply thought I was insane.

Every morning, I'd look in the mirror, lift my lip up, and see if my new tooth had arrived yet. Day after day, the same eye-sore looked back at me in the mirror. There was still a huge cavity. But I kept talking to myself, "That's okay, that's on God now. I'm busy doing my thing over here... that one's his problem".

Well, nothing happened for a couple weeks.

Then one Sunday afternoon, a lady from church offered to watch my 5 kids while I did an evening pharmacy delivery route. (It was a 4 to 6 hour delivery route delivering medicine and supplies to nursing homes all across Massachusetts). Grateful, I definitely accepted her offer.

I was flying south in the fast lane of the Everett Turnpike in Nashua, NH, en route to Massachusetts, and I happened to notice a guy walking on the side of the highway, between exits 6 and 5. Something inside me said, "Help that guy out". Responding to that 'voice' that I've heard before, I glanced over my right shoulder, and swerved my delivery van across the lanes from the left fast lane to the breakdown shoulder. He was actually hard to see, as he was walking slightly down the grade of the bank, and being dusk, it was just starting to get dark. I leaned over, reached across and rolled down the passenger window. "You okay man?"

"Yeah" he assured me, "I just ran out of gas at the Nashua Mall." I offered my assistance, and in fact drove him to his house in South Nashua, to get a gas can, and help him out. He was so impressed that I had stopped to help him, he made me give him my phone number.

I think he called 3 times. He said, "Jonny, I'm so impressed that you stopped to help me last week. I'm not going to stop calling you until you let me return the favor. Listen, I'm a dentist in Chichester, NH. I insist on returning the favor by giving you a free cleaning and exam."

I finally said, "Okay Ray, I'll come. Where's your office?"

Mind you, I'm a little thick, but I had in no way made the connection between him running out of gas and my 'prayer of faith', but during my first visit Dr. Ray said, "See that tooth Jonny, I'm going to fix that for free".

Now if you insist that that was all a mere coincidence, I don't know what to tell you, but I know full well that that was Jesus Christ (not religion) coming through for me one more time, in a big way.

And this story is not fantasy. Dr. Ray Farland of Chichester, NH remains my dentist to this very day. In fact, after I eventually told him about my prayer prior to meeting him, he'd often ask me to share with another patient or hygienist how, 'God had used him too'.

So let me encourage you, that if you are at your wit's end, and running on empty, call out to God to help you. And I don't mean some mystical 'force' in the universe, I mean the only witnessed execution by torture, witnessed by thousands, that only days later reappeared and showed himself to hundreds. It wasn't a ghost, he even ate fish with them and told them to touch him. This is not fantasy, and this is not religion. This is history.

When's the last time you sincerely called out to God for help? Has it been a while? He wants to, and promises to help when you call out to him. Of course He can pull through in the big things, even the miraculous. But how about asking Him on the way to your next enrollment, "Please God, help me do a good job presenting today" or "Please God, help me write enough policies this week to pay the rent". He hears those too.

Now here's the real secret, Dr. Ray wasn't the first person I've ever pulled over for to help. And I'm sure he won't be the last. However, there are times when I see a disabled motorist along the side of the highway and I don't stop. Maybe I'm barely on time for a big presentation, or I have a plane to catch. But even in either of those scenarios, what if I saw a stalled-out motor vehicle in the center lane of a crazy busy 5-lane highway, with rushing vehicles going by on either side at speeds in excess of 70 MPH, and suddenly I realized that the disabled motorist was one of my daughters! Now would I just pass by? Hell no!

There's a verse in the Good Book found in John that says, "To anyone who believes in Him, He gives the right to be called a child of God". And He means that literally. It doesn't say "whoever is perfect, gets baptized, or gave money to a TV preacher", but merely whoever 'believes in Him'.

In the same way God 'may' randomly help a lot of people, we hear about it all the time. But also, in the same way, God will 'never' drive by one of his kids!

And the offer to become his literal child, adopted into his family, (not figuratively), still stands for everyone. None of us will ever be 'good enough' to get close to Him, but that's why He already paid the price, on that dreadful cross.

But this father/son, father/daughter relationship starts the day you accept His offer. It's a literal adoption process. But He doesn't adopt anyone that doesn't want to be, and doesn't accept His free offer.

My dad taught me a word picture once. He said, "Son, I want you to have this quarter", as he reached out his palm displaying a shiny 25 cent coin. Naturally, like any kid, my eyes got big. I hesitated for a moment, seeing if perhaps there was a catch, but before long, reached out and snagged the prize. My dad smiled, and then asked me, "At what point did that quarter become yours'? Was it when I offered it, or was it when you reached out and took it?"

Ownership occurs when you take the conscious step to accept the offer.

God's offer still stands. Will you reach out and accept it?

The moment you do, God becomes your Daddy. Now, better than any big brother you could ask to have in your corner, you can conquer the world.

Now if you allow Him to adopt you, you've also become His child. I have no idea what your Earthly parents were like. They may have been great. They may have let you down. Regardless, God is a perfect parent.

Now that you're His child, unless there's a good reason why not to, He'll most likely give you whatever you ask for. But just remember, He's a dad and He ultimately knows best. When one of my kids asked for ice cream when they were little, there were times when I'd have to say, "Not yet". As they got a little older, I could begin to reason with them, but when they were really small, I just had to make the call. In those times, I wouldn't deny them ice cream because I 'didn't' love them…it was because I did! As a grown-up, I knew that if supper was only an hour away, a toddler with a belly full of ice cream won't eat his dinner. If I didn't have his or her best intent in mind, I could just cave in to make them happy in the moment. But in the long run, they get a stomach ache and miss their proper nourishment. That's just 'Parenting 101'.

So trust Him. With the blind faith of a child, dare to ask Him for whatever your heart desires. If it's 'good-for-you', He very well may answer your prayer right away. Other times, when He knows what's best for you, His answer might be, "Not Yet". But dare to ask Him, and then sit back and trust Him. Actually, don't just sit back, but get very busy. God acknowledges and blesses hard work, especially when there's a vision behind it. Work your butt off like it's up to you, and at the same time pray your guts out like it's up to Him. They're both right!

But develop a God-consciousness. Even in the little things throughout the day, start talking to Him…in your mind, under your breath.

Here's a few 'minute-man' prayers I've used in the past:

"God, please help me book 10 appointments today".

"God, please have the employer get all the employees in the break room for my presentation".

"God, please help me make National Convention to Hawaii!"

More often than not, your prayer will get answered. If it doesn't, trust that it's only because He's got something better in mind".

Maybe if that company hadn't rescheduled that enrollment last week, you would've written a few accident policies. But maybe God orchestrated that too, because now the owner is back in town, and because of the recent increase in the company's deductible, now he wants to offer every employee a $20/week allowance toward whatever Aflac they want.

I recommend starting every morning by asking God for His favor, and then trust Him to bless all of your efforts, day in and day out.

Now if you're not quite sure 'how' to become one of His kids, let me show you how simple it is. You can just pray a very simple prayer like, "Jesus, I admit I'm a sinner who falls short sometimes. Yet, I accept the fact that you died on the cross in my place. I know I can't earn it, and I don't deserve it, but I accept your offer to adopt me. I believe in my heart that you really did rise from the dead over 2000 years ago, and that you live forevermore. Please make me your child as of this very day. Amen."

The precise moment you said "Amen", it became official, and the adoption papers were finalized. Now you're His kid, and He's with you forever.

Now that very simple 'prayer' doesn't have to be accompanied by a priest or Rabbi. It's between you and Him. You can mutter those words while you're driving, or you can kneel down beside your bed. But do it, accept the free gift of a personal relationship with the creator of the universe.

Then, I encourage you to tell somebody. Many feel the weight of the world come off their shoulders the moment they say, "Amen". Many come to tears, and years of heartache and pain even seem to fade. Share this 'good news' with those you love, just don't add any 'religion' to the formula. God is all you need.

And if you have accepted that offer, I'd be thrilled to hear about it.

Now you and God together are forever a majority. Go conquer the world!

# Kaizen

I teach 'Kaizen' class every week. It's actually a Samurai term that means 'constant and never-ending improvement'. Always be learning. Always gets better.

And don't resist change. Like many of the strategies I went over in this book, stay on top if it, and capitalize on it. Learn to be the expert.

'Leaders are Readers'. Whether you want to lead a team, or just take the lead in the ranking reports... read!

It's barely May, and I've already read 6 books so far this year. (And I promise you that I'm no less busy than you!) Read books that challenge you, and read books that help you and dare you to dream bigger.

I also encourage you to read publications that help you keep up with all the changes in the marketplace. You definitely should subscribe to Benefits Pro, and you really need to study the Aflac Work Force Reports.

Tim Martin also has a fantastic weekly e-mail and Podcast called "Success is Voluntary". (By the way, I bet he reads 'twice' as much as I do). I believe he was an Aflac associate and Regional Manager for something like 20 years, yet his program is 'carrier neutral', and agents building a business with voluntary insurance listen in whether they represent Aflac, Allstate or Colonial. We can 'all' learn from each other.

And read books that build your faith. I read 'God Winks' in January, and I have to say it was awesome.

And definitely read books that cultivate the 'millionaire mindset'. You are who you associate with. Make it a point to 'associate' with multi-millionaires every day, by reading something they wrote.

And cling to your CIT/DSC/RSC or anyone else that is willing to help. Take every training that your Market office offers. And make it a point to get to know your Market Director.

And as I conclude this book, I again offer my personal assistance to you. If you call, I just might answer. If I don't, I promise you I will call you back, even if it takes a day or two. You will get a response. Please feel free to e-mail me as well.

Please do let me know how it's going out there. I'd love to coach you, as well as celebrate your success.

With every ounce of my being, I wish you unprecedented success.

See you at the top!

God Bless,
Jonny

Jonny Burgess
434 Donald Street
Bedford, NH 03110
(603)264-0961
jburgessrei@yahoo.com

# BONUS : Building a Million Dollar District in a Year

PART OF THE AFLAC Dream is the ability to advance, and move into management with this company. It isn't inside or political or cliquey connections that get you promoted here, it's simply the desire to take your career to another level. Simply put, if you learn how to do this business very well, and you have the desire and the ability to teach others to also do this business very well, then management may very well be for you.

Now management is not necessarily a needed step to become wealthy with Aflac. There are countless agents that love their life as an associate, and make significant 6 and even 7-figure incomes in this business. Especially with a well-serviced 'milk route' model, a $250,000 to $350,000/year income is a very realistic expectation within a decade (if not sooner).

Furthermore, what I've seen during my career is that many times managers (at various levels) reach the point that their renewals are comfortably in the 6-figure arena, even if they don't get out of bed in the morning, and many say,

"Okay, enough of that. I think I'm done.", because honestly it is a lot of additional work, and a lot of responsibility. So we can't blame them for eventually wanting to hang up the gloves so to speak, yet at the same time that does create a huge vacancy, and a desperate need for more managers.

The DSC (district sales coordinator) contract, as Dan Amos will tell you, is the most profitable contract across the board. The overrides are the highest, you receive matching first-year FireBall bonuses. There are multiple corporate sponsored contests and incentives specifically for the DSC level. The potential to maximize your annual quota and FAME bonus can result in a six-figure bonus check each February. There are additional stock bonuses. You can build up your renewals at an accelerated pace, and yet you can still write your own business, and build up your personal production, revenue, renewals, and stock at the 01 level. It's a LOT of work, as you tend to wear a lot the hats simultaneously, but it can be VERY rewarding.

And…you are drastically impacting the lives of the members of your team. You can build a team that catches your vision, and wants to jump on that train-ride to success. There's very little that's more rewarding than being on a National Convention trip, and bringing people with you!

To be transparent, it can also be heartbreaking. At times you'll want success for your people more than they want it for themselves. You'll see some very promising candidates give up on their dreams way too early, especially when it doesn't happen quite as fast as they were expecting.

Okay, let's say you've made the decision that management is for you. What's the first step?

Let me say this: "Leadership is 20% given, and 80% taken."

What I mean by that is if becoming a manager is your vision, then don't wait to be noticed, or hope someone in upper management eventually brings up the conversation. Get very pro-active immediately. Tell your DSC and/or RSC that that is your plan. Start volunteering 'now'. Ask to speak on a topic at an upcoming Monday-Morning-Meeting. Ask to take out a new recruit and have them shadow you for a day. And most importantly…start building your own team now.

Be on the constant lookout for people that you can envision being on your team. Ask that waitress that you couldn't help but notice was extremely good with people, "Say, you are great at what you do. Let me ask you, is this your career, or is it just a job for you?"

Before long, you can become a CIT (coordinator-in-training). You will begin building a team that will go with you when you are ready to take the helm as a DSC yourself.

Then, my best advice to any new district out there… lead from the front!

If your team-members picture their leader as a guy or gal with their feet up on a desk somewhere, like an armchair quarterback, it won't work, at least not for long. But if they picture you like Mel Gibson in 'Braveheart', dressed in warpaint wielding a battle-axe screaming, and the first one to charge across the field…they'll respect you, want to learn from you, and will go above and beyond to deliver not just for themselves, but for the good of the team.

So where do you start?

Let's say that it's January 1st, you're a brand-new district, and let's even say that when you look in the mirror, you are looking at your entire team. It's just you for now. Go sell somebody something! Get very busy, and at first assume that you are going to have to do it all yourself. Whether your annual quota is $200,000 or $350,000, you can move that needle an awful lot yourself.

But 'always' be on the lookout for talent. Make it part of your DNA to always have your antennas up to find people. Your RSC will be recruiting for you as well. Be grateful when you get a new recruit from your regional to work with, but for the most part...go find your team. They're out there.

A quick flashback to my "You Can Too" system as a whole...

If you make sure that 'you' do the things that you are going to expect your associates to do, they'll be much more likely to respect you, and to follow suit.

So make sure 'you'..."Book 10/Run 10".

By now, you're a Rockstar closer. If you put yourself in front of 10 small business owners each week, don't you think you'll close at least one right away?

Typically, one will close immediately, one ends up being a direct sale, and another one closes in the near future, possibly a couple weeks later. The other seven remain in the hopper and may eventually close, but focus on the quick closes, and be sure to "Book 10 more" next week.

Now, even in my rookie year, as I was perfecting my 'system', there was twice that I closed 4 accounts in a single day! But if the above expectation is achieved, and you are talking to that many business owners, do you think it's far-fetched to anticipate writing just 10 policies/week? Of course not. "3-accidents-and-out" is still at least 3 policies.

Let's say you write on average one 6-man group/week. It's pretty conservative to think that you'll write at least 10 policies, don't you think, just with an occasional upsell of a dental, vision, or life? If the average AP per/policy is $400...X's 10 policies/week...that's $4000/week. That's $200,000/year.

You're already 20% there towards a Million-Dollar-District!

Now, I recommend taking on 2 projects/quarter. That means putting your heart and soul (blood, sweat & tears) into 2 lives every 3 months. Typically, one will want it bad enough to make it work, and will want to emulate you. The other, well...you just can't make someone want it if they don't. It's sad, but for everyone's sake, when they don't measure up (and I mean desire, willingness to work, being teachable etc. much more than just immediate success out of the gate), then you need to fail 'em fast. If they're not in it 100%, don't give them your 100%. Spend your most time and energy with those that want it (almost) as bad as you do.

But after three months, you've just cloned yourself, and now there are '2' of you out there...booking 10 and running 10, and now you're up to a $400,000 district.

Next quarter, do it again. Pour your life into two others, and one of 'em will stick. After 2 quarters...that's a $600,000 district.

In Q-3, you do it again...that's $800,000.

In Q-4 you devote yourself one more time to 2 souls, and see which one wants it more.

You've just built a $1,000,000 district in 12 months! The following calendar year, your team's premium will have two commas in it!

Along the way, some of those who didn't quite see the vision, are still around. Maybe for them $1000/month is all they were after anyway, because they have another income, or a supporting spouse. But even the flash in the pans that are gone before you know it, still helped move the needle. That little bit of premium they did write still contributed to the cause. The 80/20 rule is a valid one, but that additional 20% might just multiply your year-end bonus. Those couple accounts still helped you hit your FAME metrics.

I still see names on my monthly statement that were here for a few weeks then vanished, but the override (and stock) on the little that they did is still there.

And…if they leave, you take over those accounts, and that's now another stop on your own 'milk route'.

And just how do you manage a schedule (that honestly was already full before you stepped into a management role), help more than one person at a time, take care of all the unfun back office stuff…and still manage to find time to write your own business? I can only share with you what I did, and what worked for me.

When I had a brand new agent, literally first day on the street, I'd 'start' by hitting a string of doors. Usually 10 to 20. Then I'd get a cup of coffee with them somewhere and start the training. I reiterate what I just said at those prospects, and remind them of what we just got for results, whether we booked 1 appointment or 10. Then we'd role play that opening line a few times…just the basic, "How are you? I haven't had a chance to meet you yet"…to, "You've seen the duck on TV right?"

But before we hit the street again, I'd blow their mind just a little bit with just how big my goals were, and how I now expected them to come up with their own '100'. Their next homework assignment was to pick up a copy of "Success Principles" and start developing the millionaire mindset.

Then we'd hit another ½ dozen doors…hopefully with them doing the last couple.

Then back in the car, I'd go over the game-plan, "Alright. Thursday morning we'll start with the diner and landscaper I just booked, and those could even become your first two accounts. Now your only purpose in life, between now and Thursday morning, is to get a whole lot of other people to say 'Yes' to the duck question. Book as many appointments as you can, and Thursday after the landscaper and diner, I'll run those for you too. Got it?"

And I'd kick them out of the car.

Their head should be spinning already, along with the excitement that the diner we just pitched might very well become his/her account just days from now! While they're excited, I want them hitting doors, on their own, right away. I didn't just hand them a few brochures and merely say, "Good luck, go get 'em kid". No, I modeled it for them, practiced with them, dreamed a little, and then modelled it again. Then I set the expectation.

And think about this from their point-of-view. They don't have to be overwhelmed learning every aspect of this industry. They have one purpose in life for now...book appointments. And think about what an invaluable asset they have...you! You are going to close those first few cases 'for' them, and they'll make some money immediately!

And the flip side, do you know what you have? A free appointment-setting service! Literally, if you have two agents out there doing nothing but booking appointments for you, that you are going to come back and close, how much business do you think you can write now? Can you picture the momentum?

Now what I would do is give each (new) associate on my team two 3 or 4 hour blocks of time. Maybe Sam got Tuesday afternoon from 1:00-5:00, and Friday morning from 9:00-12:00. Then Tim might get Wednesday morning 9:00 to 1:00, and Thursday afternoon from 2:00 to 5:00. In between I'd run my own stuff, conduct enrollments, or whatever else was on the endless 'to-do' list associated with management.

When I picked up that associate at 9:00am, I'd say, "Okay Joe, where's our first one?" And we were off to the races.

But what if I pulled up, Joe jumped in the car, only to find out that Joe didn't book any appointments? I can't say that never happened, but I can say it only would happen once (with the same agent). If they didn't have any appointments for us to run, just what were they doing all day since we left each other two days ago? That's when you figure out if it's call reluctance, laziness, or merely their ineffectiveness. Listen, I was always very merciful…if they were working. If they 'honestly' cold-called for two straight days, but netted no appointments…we needed to practice the script again. But really, even a blind squirrel finds an occasional nut. If they were out for two days, and were actually working, they should've booked at least a couple. But we'd roll-play again, then I'd model a few more live for them with them shadowing me, then cut them loose again. If Friday morning, they 'again' had no appointments…we'd have a hard conversation. I'd remind them that I was on a mission to become wealthy, and that one of my life goals was to help 5 other people become millionaires too. If they don't want to be one of them, I've got to spend my time with people who do.

If they fought for the right to be one of my 5…I'd give them one more chance. But they knew as hard as I worked, I was much too serious about my future to waste time with people who weren't serious.

Though it still hurt when people didn't want it bad enough for themselves.

The last advice I'd give, is instill the dream in each member of the team. Make sure they come up with their own '100', and find out what drives them. Remind them often.

I'd slowly work myself out of a job over time. At first, they just book the appointments, and I took over from there. Before long, I'd have them run a couple of ERs themselves. (I would recommend running their first solo presentations on something like a convenience store owner that might not even have employees. Don't have them 'practice' on a 12-life case! You run all those for now). But soon they have the ER down as well, and you're just coming in to do the employee presentation, or assist with the enrollment. Before long (about 13 weeks) they should be pretty self-sufficient, and I can now invest my energy into the next hungry newbie or two.

But make sure you are always a life-life, just a phone call away.

Do an occasional lunch & learn for yourself to make sure no matter how busy you get, you keep the cash flow coming.

And don't be afraid to invest in your business. It'll come back to you many times over.

People flock to people with a vision. Go bring out the best in them!

# Recommended Reading List

*The Success Principles* by Jack Canfield

*Think & Grow Rich* by Napolean Hill

*Millionaire Mindset* by Harv Eker

*The Magic of Thinking Big* by David J. Schwartz

*The Blessed Life* by Robert Morris

*The Aladdin Factor* by Jack Canfield and Mark Victor Hanson

*Your Best Life Now* by Joel Osteen

*Awaken the Giant Within* by Anthony Robbins

*You Can, You Will* by Joel Osteen

*The 5 Love Languages* by Gary Chapman

*Write it Down, Make it Happen* by Henriette Anne Klauser

*What Wives Wish Their Husbands Knew About Women* by James Dobson

*The Signature of God* by Dr. Grant Jeffries

*Creation* by Dr. Grant Jeffries

*Personality Plus* by Florence Littauer

*When God Winks at You* by Squire Rushnell

*More Than a Carpenter* by Josh McDowell

*Heaven is For Real* by Lynn Vincent and Todd Burpo

*The Holy Bible recommended...* New Living Translation

*Rich Dad/Poor Dad* by Robert Kiyosaki

*The Retirement Miracle* by Patrick Kelly

*How to Reach Your Life Goals* by Peter Daniels

*Debt Free For Life* by David Bach

*Extreme Ownership* by Leif Babin and Jacko Willink

*The Coaching Principles* by Jack Canfield and Mark Victor Hanson

*4DX (the 4 Disciplines of Execution)* by Sean Covey

*Stocks Market Miracles* by Wade Cook

*The Greatest Salesman in the World* by Og Mandino

*How I Raised Myself From Failure to Success in Selling* by Frank Bettger

# Most Recent Success Story

KRISTA PRUE, MENTIONED EARLIER in this book, was recently challenged. With "zero" sales experience, and a dreadful fear of public speaking, Krista proved that "You Can Too", by writing over $500,000 AP and 52 new accounts in her first year.

Two year later, just back from President's Club as well as territory convention in Miami... just last week went to 43 doors, and booked 40 appointments... many already set up to enroll!

She just wrote $109,000 in 4 weeks!

Guess what?

**YOU CAN TOO!**

# About the Author

Born and raised in southern New Hampshire, Jonny Burgess was the baby of six kids, raised by a father who was an electrical engineer at MIT, and a very busy stay-at-home mom (former nurse), who cared for and raised not only her six, but countless nieces, nephews, foster kids, and a slew of other kids over the years that needed love, security, and a modeled life of faith.

Ambitious from his earliest childhood, Jonny finished top-10 running cross-country in NH while still in junior-high, before starting his long career in martial arts at the age of 13. Operating his first karate school (while still in high school), by age 18 had already begun competing internationally, and all across the U.S. by the time he graduated.

An unplanned pregnancy toward the end of high school shifted his life's course for a season... working 5 jobs at times, and having 5 children by the time he was 25.

Before long, Jonny reopened his karate school, built it up to 120 students, and began to compete again, regionally.

Then in July of 1999, a drunk driver ran Jonny's van off the road. He hit a tree head-on, and rolled down the embankment, severely injuring his back, breaking a vertebra. Unable to walk (never-mind work) without a cane or walker for 7 months, Jonny lost everything, including his house, and had to start all over again.

No longer able to perform the martial arts professionally, due to his injuries, Jonny started a package-delivering service in and around the Boston market.

Through another series of unfortunate events, Jonny ended up with full custody of his 5 children, and found himself a single father.

Eventually, Jonny got involved in gourmet food sales, and before long found himself managing a sales force for a national food-service company.

Then in 2008, as the economy started tanking, his food sales began to plummet. Seeing the handwriting on the wall, this single dad had to find a way to start over once again.

Jonny's 2nd wife (fiancé at the time) Michelle introduced him to some friends who were involved with Aflac. The Regional Sales Manager (and eventual Market Director) Bill Henry gave him an opportunity... and Jonny flourished.

Opening 72 accounts in his first 11 months, Jonny went on to be the #1 account opener in the U.S. in his rookie year (2009), as he developed his "system".

After being promoted to DSC, Jonny began assembling his team, and led them on a record-setting pace, and in 2012 finished the #1 DSC in the country, opening 241 accounts.

Jonny's first book, *You Can Too*, detailed his early success, and taught his "system". Soon after, he was asked to speak in multiple states across the country in front of countless district, regional, and state teams.

Now an RSC in NH, Jonny currently manages 8 districts, while continuing to teach and coach his system across the country.

Jonny and his wife Michelle blended their families back in 2009, and together raised 8 kids, but today enjoy an "empty nest" as the youngest is away in her 3rd year of college. Now proud grandparents to 7 (and counting), Jonny and Michelle proved that you can overcome *any* obstacles that come your way, and live the life of your dreams. And they'll tell you that "You Can Too!"

*"I have read and re-read the book several times. I found the book inspirational, instructional, motivational, and the last chapter on faith, sealed the deal for me.*

*My training and support has been second to none at Aflac, and I still find the book very valuable.*

*Mr. Burgess, if you ever wonder if you can change people's lives...you can, and I am sure I am one of many."*

—David R. (North Carolina)

CPSIA information can be obtained
at www.ICGtesting.com
Printed in the USA
BVHW081732110319
542317BV00001B/148/P